CHRISTMAS CRACKER

By the same author:

The Complete Youth Manual Volume 1

Christmas Cracker

STEVE CHALKE

KINGSWAY PUBLICATIONS
EASTBOURNE

Front cover photos by Jim Loring

British Library Cataloguing in Publication Data

Chalke, Steve
  Christmas cracker.
  1. Charities. Fund raising
  I. Title
  361.70681.

  ISBN 0-86065-551-2

Printed in Great Britain for
KINGSWAY PUBLICATIONS LTD
1 St Anne's Road, Eastbourne, E Sussex BN21 3UN by
Richard Clay Ltd, Bungay, Suffolk
Typeset by Nuprint Ltd, Harpenden, Herts

Contents

This book is dedicated
to
Cornelia, Emily, Daniel, Abigail and Joshua,
the people I love the most and who gave the
most to make Christmas Cracker
more than a dream.

My thanks to *21CC* magazine and Elm House Christian Communications Ltd for allowing my articles written for *21CC* to be included in this volume; to Gordon O'Neill, the Project Administrator of Christmas Cracker, for all his help—especially in the writing of the Bible studies; to Jenny Taylor, our Press and Publicity Officer, for writing Chapter 8 in Part One; to the Christmas Cracker Trustees and all the staff at Oasis.

INTRODUCTION
The How and Why of Christmas Cracker

In December 1983 a Christian youth group in the south of England opened a restaurant in temporary premises on the high street. They wanted to make a lot of money. Not for themselves, but to help their brothers and sisters in India. They had heard about a famine and wanted to bring water to a village.

It cost about £1,000 to drill a well. They decided that a unique kind of restaurant might raise the money.

'Why not sell third-world food at posh western prices?' they said. 'People will pay more to eat less.'

They organised their parents and friends. They wooed local businesses. A landlord lent them a vacant shop. Someone else provided rice, flour and a cooker.

When the doors opened, their enthusiasm spread to the customers. By the end of the first week's trading some people were paying five pounds for a glass of water. The restaurant started to attract attention as well as money. Regional radio did a story, which was picked up by national radio and then by television. Christmas shoppers queued for a small chicken curry or beans on toast.

The young people were thrilled. They increased the target to two wells. Local churches woke up, the community rallied to help, important issues were discussed and everyone learned a lot. In the end five wells were drilled. For everyone involved Christmas giving took on a new meaning.

In 1988 I visited India, and as a result of the poverty and suffering I saw there, alongside the heroic efforts of Indian

Christians to tackle the problems facing their country, I realised it was time to launch 'Eat less—pay more' restaurants on a national scale. Through the pages of *21CC* magazine I wrote month by month advising youth groups around the UK on how to set up their own 'Christmas Cracker' (as the restaurants now became called) over Christmas 1989.

The critics said it was ridiculous and would never work. But young people took hold of the idea and in 1989 almost 20,000 of them were involved in running 100 restaurants through the month of December, and over two hundred other one-day Cracker events. These ranged from selling food in the high street on trolleys, to mince pie stalls in shopping centres and one-day cafes in schools, village halls and churches. In fact all sorts of ideas along the lines of the 'Eat less—pay more' principle.

The result was that nearly £½ million was raised for Christian third world relief and development agencies.

Now you can be part of Christmas Cracker. We are planning to do it all again in Britain—and we hope that it will soon take off in other nations too. Run by Oasis Trust and *21CC* magazine (published by Elm House Christian Communications Ltd), the scheme is also backed by Tear Fund and Interserve, both of whom are involved in mission to the third world.

As last year all funds raised will be channelled through Christmas Cracker Trust, a new charity set up by Elm House Christian Communications Ltd and Oasis. Funds will go to existing Christian relief and development agencies and from there on to individual projects. Support will be given to established projects run by national Christians. Our goal is simply to help the third-world church in the work it is already doing.

All projects supported will have an emphasis on the needs of the whole person—physical, social and spiritual.

This book contains all you need to get going. A wise friend of mine once commented: 'Never just tell them how, make sure you tell them why!' If you simply teach young people how but not why, then when the how changes they have nothing to give. But if they understand why they do what they do, then they are in a completely different league.

Part One of this book deals with how to set up a Christmas Cracker restaurant, from publicity to planning permission, from decorating the shop to witnessing to your faith.

Part Two deals with why, not how. It contains an eleven-week teaching course designed to change young people's thinking and give them a God-sized view of the world. Karl Marx said: 'Philosophers have only interpreted the world. The point, however, is to change it.' To understand why is of little value unless you are prepared to take action.

These studies are vital because, when even the most successful restaurant is shut and the press have long since turned their attention to other things, there will be an army of young people who will be more equipped, more ready and more able to serve God for the years ahead.

STEVE CHALKE
Director, Oasis Trust

PART ONE

Christmas Cracker—Here's How

1

Motivating Young People to World Concern

Tony Campolo claims that too often 'we in youth work have mistakenly assumed that the best way to relate to young people is to provide them with various forms of entertainment.... We would do better if we invited our young people to accept the challenge to heroically change the world.' (Quoted in Paul Borthwick, *Youth and Missions*, Victor Books.)

This book is designed to challenge and equip youth leaders to give the young people in their groups a global vision, and to take seriously our responsibility to create in them a desire to 'heroically change the world'. But much more than that, the following chapters will be providing a practical step-by-step guide filled with information, advice, help and teaching material. The best learning is always linked with the opportunity to put principle into practice. Therefore, the most effective teaching about World Mission will be that which presents the opportunity to change the way things are.

The Christmas Cracker project is not expensive, it doesn't require outstanding genius or rare skills and it doesn't involve travelling because it takes place in the heart of your town. Also it is not dependent on the size of your group—no matter how large or small, any group can be involved. What it does require, however, is vision, imagination and the desire to change the world in which we live.

A mission to destroy boring Christianity

In 1954 Billy Graham visited Great Britain for the first time to lead a crusade at Haringey which met with staggering success. In the face of this Billy thought very seriously about the possibility of staying in Britain for a much longer period but eventually decided to return home.

Years later David Frost wrote, wondering what would have happened if Billy had stayed, 'Would we have become a nation as dull and narrow-minded as some of his followers, or a nation as vibrantly alive and fragrantly Christian as Dr Graham himself?...I wish he'd stayed.' That statement cuts deep. That followers of Jesus Christ, the most dynamic man who has ever walked the face of the earth, should be labelled as 'dull'! And yet our own experience tells us that so often this is only too true. As the church becomes inward-looking and we pile words upon more words, the spiritual lives of many Christians both young and old can quite rightly be described as dull, mundane, stale, routine, stagnant, empty and barren. Why? Because they are not given the opportunity to step out and get involved. Or they don't take it.

Jesus called twelve ordinary people to follow him. They weren't 'super-heroes' or 'giants of faith' but they were willing to trust him. What's more, he didn't insist that they got themselves a diploma from the local theological college before taking them on board. It wasn't that Jesus thought it was unimportant to believe the right things, but he knew it was only as the disciples got involved 'on the frontline' that they would ever really begin to learn and grow in spiritual maturity.

The worst sermon Jesus ever preached?

Matthew 25:31–46 contains one of the most challenging and controversial sermons Jesus ever preached. It's all about the last judgement when all men and women shall appear before him to give account of themselves. In it Jesus talks about the basis for his judgement on individuals and how he plans to separate 'the sheep from the goats'. But if Jesus were a modern-day preacher, this kind of message wouldn't go down too well in most evangelical churches! He definitely wouldn't be asked to preach again and in fact may well be shouted down half-way through or, at very least, given a serious talking to by some of the elders after the service.

The problem is that Jesus clearly states judgement will take place on the basis of what we 'did' rather than what we 'believed'. 'I was hungry and you fed me, thirsty and you gave me a drink, I was a stranger and you received me...naked and you clothed me; I was sick and you took care of me.' What's more, though Jesus engages in this penetrating analysis of the lives of those who appear before him, he never mentions—even in passing—the matter of whether they have ever prayed a prayer of forgiveness or seen a copy of 'the four spiritual laws'. It's clear that for Jesus faith without works is dead, and that the only real way to test if faith exists at all is to put it into action. It's impossible to avoid this obvious but far-reaching implication of Jesus' teaching.

As youth leaders it's our God-given responsibility to challenge and enable the teenagers we work with to get involved in serving Christ and the world in which we live. This book, and the whole Christmas Cracker project, will give you the opportunity of helping them do just that.

2

The Aims of Christmas Cracker

Let's face it, most teenagers are fed up with sponsored walks, swims, knits, runs, jogs, discos and silences. It's all been done too many times before. To be honest, it's all so predictable, run-of-the-mill, and lacking imagination. Christian teenagers, like all other young people, are looking for a challenge big enough to harness their energy, fire their imagination and stretch their faith. Unfortunately, rather than challenging teenagers we in the church have all too often been guilty of quenching their enthusiasm with projects and programmes so pedestrian that, far from communicating a sense of God's greatness, speak only of our lack of vision and smallness of faith. As a result their energy has been diverted into other causes, because their experience of being a Christian and part of the church continually frustrates them. At the same time the image presented to teenagers outside the church is tame, safe and docile. If you're looking for a lifestyle that's remotely challenging the clear message is: 'Don't ask the church about it!'

Christmas Cracker is designed to give your youth group the opportunity of becoming part of a national project

which will challenge and motivate them as they trust God
and get involved. At the same time it will let your town and
our country know loud and clear that becoming a Christian
brings you to life not puts you to sleep!

In 1989 Christmas Cracker's target was to set up a chain
of at least 200 temporary restaurants using empty high-
street shops around the UK all selling 'Eat Less—Pay
More' food. Because much of the food was donated, all the
money taken in the tills was channelled through established
Christian agencies to the church on the Indian sub-continent for use in their existing relief and development projects among the poor and the weak.

Over all, there are six impact areas Christmas Cracker
was designed to hit:

(1) The nations receiving aid

Our first target nation was India, which has been labelled
'the forgotten third world'. It is the second-most populated
nation on earth (only China has more people) and by the
year 2000 it will have more than a billion (that is, a thousand million) people. It is currently going through the crisis
of urbanisation, with millions flocking each year from the
villages to the big cities in the vain hope of finding work.
The vast majority of these people end up living in shanty
towns or on the pavements with no hope and no future. In
India as a whole one in every ten children die before their
first birthday; in the slum areas this is often as high as one in
two. Only 30% of the urban population have any access to
sanitation; in rural areas it's just 1%. Two-thirds of the
entire adult population can't read. Many children never
have the opportunity of schooling, and only 35% reach
secondary education.

We set up a new charitable trust called 'The Christmas
Cracker Trust' which acted as a clearing house to channel
the money raised, to established Christian relief and
development agencies for use in the countries which make

up the Indian sub-continent (besides India itself that includes Bangladesh, Pakistan, Nepal and Sri Lanka).

(2) The church in the nation receiving aid

The church in India faces a massive challenge. A lot is already being done, in fact we have a great deal to learn from the initiatives that are being taken. The problem is that the task is so great that it cannot possibly be tackled effectively without our help. It's not new ideas that the Indian church needs; it's our enthusiastic support for the work in which it's already involved. But we need to remember that when we give our support it's not a case of one organisation generously doing another a favour, it's simply one big family using its resources to meet the needs of all its members.

(3) Your youth group

The aid which is given is not the whole story—there's a lot more to Christmas Cracker than that. Running a local restaurant will not only help meet needs overseas—it will also make a big impact here in our own country.

Part Two of this book provides a pre-Christmas syllabus for your group that examines what it means to be a world Christian. The studies unpack the Great Commission and world mission in a relevant, thought-provoking way, as well as tackling tough questions like 'What happens to those who've never heard?' and 'Why does God allow suffering?' Running the restaurant in December then provides a way of giving your group the opportunity to respond to some of what they've learnt in the preceding months.

Maybe you don't feel your group has the resources to set up and operate a Christmas Cracker on its own, so why not work together with other churches in your town? Unless you live in a very big town it doesn't make sense to run two restaurants anyway! When you register with the national Christmas Cracker organisation, you'll find out about any other groups interested in the project in your town, so you can get in touch.

(4) Your church

History and personal experience tell us that real unity is only discovered and developed when there's a challenge to be faced. Though your youth group will launch and manage the Christmas Cracker, when it comes to staffing it they will need the help of the rest of the church. The youth group will be able to staff the restaurant in the evenings and on Saturdays and cope with a lot of the daytime work once the holidays have started, but a rota of adult volunteers to help with weekday staffing is essential.

This creates an ideal opportunity for any adult church members who are available during the day to get involved. Added to this, there may be church members with useful skills which will be a great help as you set up—for example a signwriter, printer, electrician, painter-and-decorator, or grocer.

(5) Your town

Imagine the impact of a restaurant run by your youth group serving meals, snacks and drinks in the middle of the high street throughout the Christmas shopping period. Think of the added potential of being one in a chain of similar restaurants operating at the same time under the same name across the country. Think of the press coverage through newspapers and radio; of the talking point the project will create at school gates, in office and factory canteens between staff, in other shops in the town. Running a Christmas Cracker restaurant will make your youth group the talk of the town over Christmas, and this will raise awareness of our responsibility to the Third World, channel the resulting funds into Christian hands, and also create one of the best evangelistic opportunities your youth group and church have ever had.

(6) Our nation

In 1983 running one restaurant in Tonbridge in the south-east of England won national media coverage on radio, in magazines and newspapers as well as on regional TV. In 1989 the impact of a chain of restaurants, all under the same name, run by Christian young people across the country, caught the whole nation's attention through the enthusiastic interest shown by national TV, radio and newspapers. This time you can be involved.

How to get involved

Register your youth group at the Christmas Cracker office and they'll send you a *What Now?* leaflet with more information. There is a form at the back of this book.

Order a copy of the Christmas Cracker promotional video, 'A Different Kind of Giving', filmed in India, Uganda and the UK. It will inspire your group to get involved, and is available from the office who will also advise you of the current price.

3

Getting Organised

How to get the right shop

Getting the right shop is the key to Christmas Cracker. With it you're on your way to making a big impact on your town, without it the whole project is little more than a daydream. Obtaining the use of a shop may at first seem a rather daunting task, but like most other problems it's simply a matter of knowing what to do and when to do it. To make life easier for you, the central office is geared up to do as much of this work as possible.

Christmas Cracker gets involved in negotiations with several major national chains of estate agents and seeks their help to ensure that suitable empty properties are made available for use at Christmas. Sometimes the central office will even be able to do all the negotiating for you— all you'll have to do is pick up the keys and move in! But if it's not possible to obtain a property for you through their national contacts, they'll give you all the help you need to negotiate with local agencies.

And remember, if a shop is not available at all, a high-street church front or community hall would make a great Christmas Cracker, given a little creative thought.

Shop premises are a great financial asset but also a costly liability if they stand empty for too long. Therefore you can guarantee that the owner is doing his best to sell as quickly as possible. So in most cases it won't be until three or four weeks before you want to move in that a shop's owner is likely to be willing to give you a firm commitment. Be prepared not to have final confirmation of the availability of a shop until mid-October or even early November.

Remember that because the question of which shop you will be able to use cannot be firmed up until the last minute, everything else needs to be organised well in advance so that you're not suddenly plunged into the ironic situation where, having obtained a shop, you're not organised enough to do anything with it!

More detailed advice on finding premises is contained in Chapter 5.

The Cracker line

Whatever problems you run up against, help is only a phone call away if you are in Britain. The special telephone help-line is in operation during the autumn to provide you with all the extra advice and back-up you need. Registration with the project gives you access to this number and expert help whenever you require it.

How to build a team

It's vital to the success of your local Christmas Cracker that the members of your youth group really feel it belongs to them. Don't try to steal ownership for yourself or allow other members of your church to take the project over in an attempt to organise it for the teenagers.

Your role is to guide, advise and 'carry the can', but at the same time allow the youth group as much responsibility as possible. There are four steps you need to take now to enthuse your group to launch a Christmas Cracker restaurant.

1. Show them the Christmas Cracker video.

2. Get them to begin praying about the project on a regular basis.

3. Enthuse them about the teaching course which should run from September until the project begins at the end of November (see Part Two of this book).

4. Appoint suitable young people to the various roles that need to be filled: *General Manager, *Accountant/ Cashier, *Chief Chef, *Kitchen Team, *Head Waiter, *Team of waiters and waitresses, *Press and publicity Officer, *Churches Liaison Officer, *Maintenance and decoration crew.

The following chapters outline the role each person will play in the development of the project.

Setting a financial target

In 1983 when we ran the original 'Eat Less—Pay More' restaurant in Tonbridge we set the target figure we wanted to raise at £1,000. We actually passed that target in just over one week, and so reset our sights on £4,000. Several of the restaurants run in 1989 raised nearly £10,000, and many others well over £5,000.

Sit down with your group and talk about setting your own target. Make sure it's just beyond what you think is attainable; that way you have a real challenge on your hands. But don't set one which is unrealistic or, instead of encouraging faith and commitment, it is likely to have the opposite effect and actually demotivate your group.

Budget

It's difficult to prepare an exact budget for the project at the early stages. In Tonbridge we launched the original restaurant with a gift of £50 and still had five pounds left when we opened. Almost all of the equipment we needed was donated, or loaned free of charge to us by local businesses.

As the project gained momentum we were able to obtain everything from cash registers, microwaves, fridges and freezers, to paint, cutlery, tables and chairs, as well as printing services and publicity.

Local traders will want to help—they simply need to be approached in the correct way. In a later chapter I'll be explaining exactly how to go about approaching local sponsors. Perhaps there are those in your church who will be willing to make a gift or a loan to help you set up the project. Alternatively there may already be funds available in your youth group budget.

The setting-up costs you will incur are not great but are likely to include:

* The production and duplication of a regular prayer letter.

* When you register, Christmas Cracker will ask you for £10 to cover the cost of mailings and resources which will be made available to you through the year.

* The cost of the Christmas Cracker video.

* There are high-quality brochures available which explain the project for local businesses, to win their support and sponsorship. These are available at cost price. Again, the central office can give details.

* Later in the year posters, menu cards etc are available.

* T-shirts, Christmas cards and other merchandise are also
  available later in the year, for sale in your restaurant.

Because your local Christmas Cracker is part of a
national project and is raising money for relief work, it is
likely to attract a good deal of media attention. It is therefore essential to keep a proper set of accounts. Any financial outlay can be deducted from your total income, but you
must keep invoices with your records.

4

The Cracker Countdown

This chapter introduces 'The Cracker Countdown', an outline for an eleven-week teaching programme on world mission. The actual content of the course is to be found in Part
Two. The Cracker Countdown is an essential part of your
youth group's preparation for running a restaurant and is
designed to provide a solid and exciting basis to the whole
project. The best time to run it is from the beginning of
September to the end of November when the restaurant
opens.

The Cracker Countdown

Week 1: What is the Christmas Cracker?

An introduction to the national project and your youth
group's part in it.

Week 2: What kind of God is he? (John 1:1–14)

Aim: To show that God is an outgoing 'missionary' God.
Throughout history he has constantly involved himself with
his creation and mankind, supremely in Jesus, the Word of
God. What does this phrase mean?

Week 3: What kind of people should we be? (1 Peter 2: 9–12)

Aim: To answer the question, 'Is mission an optional extra?' To explain that God has always chosen his people to be his representatives and reflect his character as a 'light' to the nations. This was firstly true of Israel, then of Jesus and now of the church, Christ's body.

Week 4: What is world mission? (Luke 4:14–30)

Aim: To understand world mission in the light of Jesus' statement about the breadth of the gospel and his task on earth. To look at the reception given to him and his message in Nazareth.

Week 5: What can I do? (Luke 5:1–11, 27–32)

Aim: To look at the sort of people Jesus calls to serve him as well as those to whom they are sent. To show how individuals can get involved in the task of world mission through prayer, giving and going.

Week 6: What do missionaries do? (Luke 10:1–4, 25–37)

Aim: To answer the question, 'Do we feed the hungry or preach to them?' To show that the true role of the missionary overseas is to work in partnership with the national church as they meet the needs of the whole person—physical, social and spiritual.

Week 7: The reality of mission (Luke 8:1–15)

Aim: To face the realities of mission and evangelism worldwide by looking at Jesus' parable of the sower.

Week 8: What if I stay? (Luke 12:13–34)

Aim: To understand what the Bible teaches about possessions, commitment to God and our responsibilities to the poor and weak by looking at the story of the rich fool.

Week 9: Is Christianity the only way? (John 14:6–14)

Aim: To answer the questions, 'Do all religions lead to God?', 'How do we know Christianity is the right way?' and 'What right have we got to "push" Christianity on people or "spoil" their culture?'

Week 10: Power for mission (Acts 1:1–9; 2:1–13)

Aim: To grasp the full significance of the role of the Holy Spirit for mission and evangelism.

Week 11: Prayer Concert

Aim: To show your youth group that corporate prayer is not the frightening thing they thought, nor need it be boring. God can use it to touch the lives of people even thousands of miles away.

Staffing your restaurant

If getting hold of a shop is the biggest problem you face, the next one is the question of who is going to run it when the youth group members are all busy at school or work.

Though the Christmas Cracker is a youth project it offers your church the exciting opportunity to get young and not-so-young working together. The generation gap is one of those problems that often soaks up hour after hour of discussion time, but experience shows us that it never solves the problem. What's needed is a shared goal which produces a real commitment to working together. During day-time hours before the Christmas holidays begin, your youth group needs the help of adult members of your church to staff the restaurant.

It is a good idea to circulate a regular news and prayer letter (see next chapter) to keep your church well informed about the progress of the project. Why not use it to ask for offers of help with staffing? There will be all sorts of people who may be able to give a couple of hours a week or more to help you out in this way. Rota sheets are also worth while—you can use them in your church so that those interested can sign up for service! Staffing levels will vary slightly according to the exact size of your restaurant, but for an average high-street shop you will need two waitresses or waiters and two kitchen staff joined by an extra kitchen worker at the lunch-time peak period. Evenings and Saturdays definitely call for all hands on deck for the youth group.

Where will the money go?

All money raised through the Christmas Cracker restaurants goes to relief and development work in third-world countries. *21CC* magazine and Oasis have formed an Executive Committee responsible for drawing up a list of individual projects to be supported.

Alternative Crackers—a Sunday special

Some youth groups may decide that though it's not possible for them to run a restaurant they still want to get involved. 'Is there some way in which we can still be part of the project, use the teaching course and help raise funds for the third-world church?' The answer is yes.

If you are in this situation why not get your youth group to organise a special Christmas Cracker lunch on one of the Sundays just before Christmas. Invite the whole church along and get them to pay as much as they like for the meal you've prepared. Christmas Cracker will supply you with all the help and advice you need, plus suggested menus, invitation cards, posters, T-shirts and much more. Or what about an end of term school meal organised by the Christian Union?

5

Finding Premises

In a project like Christmas Cracker finding suitable premises is the biggest hurdle. Experience has shown that it is likely to be a last-minute affair. Estate agents want to sell their client's property and are therefore unwilling to release a shop too early. It is only when they know that it will not sell before Christmas that they will ask their clients if it can be used for temporary purposes.

There are various ways in which you can go about trying to find a shop.

(1) Local estate agents

By and large local estate agents will not handle commercial properties. Their business is usually more to do with residential properties. However, they will handle some properties that could suit your purposes, or at the very least they will be able to point you in the direction of someone who does.

(2) Chartered surveyors

These are more likely to handle commercial properties. You will have to look for these in your local telephone directory as very few will have offices in the high street.

(3) Property developers

These are big companies that build new developments such as shopping centres. It is therefore possible that they have new properties that have yet to be let, or empty properties that are awaiting redevelopment. Some of these companies have local offices but most are based in large cities and many are in London. The department to which you should address your enquiry will be something like The Property Services Dept, although this title may vary.

(4) Building societies

Most of the major building societies have property departments, some even have 'charity lets' departments. You will need to write to their head office or regional head office. Generally they are used to dealing with charity causes and will be reasonably sympathetic to your cause providing you can assure them your intentions are honourable. They will be particularly keen to see that it is more than just one church that is undertaking the venture. They are not so keen to be seen supporting one particular denomination. They will probably ask you to sign an agreement which sets out the terms under which you are using the shop.

(5) Charity shops service

This is a service that will, in return for a fee, endeavour to find a shop for you. They are in touch with the major building societies and other property owners who are willing to let charities use their shops. The address of the service is: Charity Shops Service, The Forge, High Street, Alconbury, Huntingdon PE17 5DS.

(6) Local council

Your local council could be the largest property owner in the district, and may be able to help you. Either find out the department relevant to your needs and approach them, or go to your local councillor and explain your situation and enlist his or her help. If you know someone in your church, or a contact in another church, who is a local councillor or involved in council work, try to enlist their help.

(7) Footslogging

This entails going out on the streets of your community and tracking down all the suitable vacant properties. When you find one, note down the address and what it was previously used for, and the agent who is handling the property. Armed with this information you can then approach them and ask about its availability.

Sometimes there is no agent's board displayed. If this is the case you could ask the neighbours if they know who the owners are and how you can get in touch with them. If they cannot help, then your local council may be able to. This method is time-consuming and can be frustrating, but it may well yield fruit.

(8) Local newspapers and local contacts

Your local newspaper may take up your cause and through its pages appeal for the use of a property. If they don't take it up you might consider running an advert in the property section of the paper. You could also try the free local property news, if your area has one. Obviously this involves expense and you will have to judge whether it is worth while.

Another way is to spread the word around. The churches in your town will have all kinds of people in all kinds of professions. They just might have the one contact that will lead you to your shop.

The right kind of approach

It is vital that when you approach any of the above you do so in the right way. Letters are a good introduction, particularly if you are dealing with an office in another town.

Make sure that you put all the relevant information in the letter. Never rely solely on letters however; a follow-up phone call or even better a personal visit is always likely to yield more results. If at all possible try to get to see the owner of the property in question. It's your enthusiasm which will sell the project.

These are some of the questions that they are likely to ask.

(1) Who are you?

Tell them about the churches involved, your particular role (secretary, committee member, etc) and the charity concerned. Remember that as a national project Christmas Cracker produces a brochure which explains the concept of the project, and also explains where the money will be going.

(2) What do you want?

The use of a property for a set period of time. Christmas Cracker 1990 runs for the four weeks prior to Christmas. The first week will be spent in preparing the property for use. No changes will be made to the fabric of the property without the express permission of the owner.

Ideally you will want a shop that has been used previously for the sale and consumption of food—preferably with all of the fittings intact. If at all possible you would like it fairly central. Of course it does not have to be a shop, it could be a hotel, a public house, or even an empty office with kitchen facilities. The important thing is not to limit yourself to 'a high street shop'. Obviously there are ideal shops but in order to obtain a property you may need to compromise a little.

(3) What provisions will you be making?

It is your responsibility to make sure that the property is adequately insured for your use. As a national project

Christmas Cracker negotiates cover for all participating restaurants. This cover includes public indemnity against accidents that happen to the general public due to your negligence while they are using the restaurant; insurance for those working in the restaurant; cover for landlords' fixtures and fittings; plate-glass windows; money on the premises or in transit; and equipment that you bring onto the premises. The property is also covered for fire insurance if a fire is started as a result of your negligence.

You will also have to undertake that you will contact any other agencies that need to know about your situation (e.g. fire, environmental health, planning department).

(4) What will we get out of it?

The brochure from Christmas Cracker will explain the benefits of business sponsorship. Their name will be carried on menu covers and displayed in the shop and on posters. Obviously as the project is given coverage by the media their names will be linked with an exciting positive project. You could also offer them posters that say something to the effect of 'We're supporting Christmas Cracker' for them to display.

Local authority planning permission

Unless your premises were used previously for the sale and consumption of food you will need to get some kind of permission from your local authority planning department. The person you need to contact is the local planning officer or assistant planning officer. Write and explain your situation fully and then follow this up where at all possible with a visit. When you register you'll be given a sample letter to adapt and use. Here again it is useful if you have a contact within council circles who will be able to advise you and who could speak on your behalf.

Getting planning permission for any shop can be difficult

and would normally take up to three months to come through. It is vital, therefore, that you explain your situation fully to the planning officer. Our experience has been that they are quite willing to help once they know the nature of the project. Personal contact seems to be the key to overcoming the many difficulties that there can be regarding planning permission.

It is important to emphasise that you are not trying to establish a restaurant permanently but only for a short period and therefore permission can be granted on a temporary basis. Normally restaurants pose two other problems which do not apply to a Christmas Cracker:

(1) Cooking fumes. Whereas normally a restaurant would need expensive ducts etc to cope with cooking fumes, in the case of a Christmas Cracker this should not be necessary as equipment will be small scale. Take a list of the equipment you intend to use and say you will be willing to accept a condition on your planning permission restricting you to that equipment.

(2) Late night opening. Christmas Crackers will not be operating late at night, so are unlikely to disturb local residents. Tell the planning department what your closing time will be and again say that you will accept a condition restricting you to this.

You should ask how quickly your application is likely to be determined and, if necessary, whether your application can be expedited so that you can get planning permission in time for the restaurant to be opened.

In some instances you may be advised that you are unlikely to get planning permission for your property or that an application cannot be determined within the short period left. In such a case it may unfortunately be necessary for you to withdraw from your Christmas Cracker project. An application for planning permission is expensive (£76 in

1990), so clearly it does not make sense to spend money on an application that is unlikely to be successful. If you are experiencing difficulties in dealing with a planning authority and would appreciate independent advice in this respect, contact the Christmas Cracker office and they may be able to put you in touch with somebody who can help.

As well as requiring planning permission, certain advertisements you might wish to display on your Christmas Cracker might require permission from the planning department. To avoid the need for this, it is probably best to restrict the scale of advertising to that which does not require consent. In Britain this means:

On shop premises—non-illuminated advertisements no more than 4.6 metres off the ground or below the bottom of first-floor windows (whichever is lower) on walls with shop windows, provided no letter, character or symbol is less than 0.75 metres high.

On churches or church halls—an advertisement of 0.6 square metres provided it is not more than 4.6 metres off the ground.

Some parts of the country are designated 'Areas of Special Control' where slightly different rules apply. Your local planning department will advise you if you are within one of these.

If you want to publicise your project more widely you can use posters up to 0.6 square metres which can be displayed with permission on church noticeboards, other shops, houses, etc at a height of up to 4.6 metres. It must be emphasised that fly posting, i.e. pasting posters on empty shops, lamp posts, etc is illegal.

It may well be that your local council will waive their rules as it is a charity project, so do ask them to be kind to you.

Alternatives to shops

It is possible that you will draw a blank in trying to find a shop. But don't give up here. There are some alternatives that you might like to pursue.

(1) Portacabin

In 1989 two groups opened up their restaurants in Portacabins. These can be hired from a local contractor. You may be able to get one donated or negotiate a reduced rate for its hire. You will have to find a suitable site, and get permission from the local council. Portacabins are also generally very small so you will not be able to fit in many customers at any one time. You will have to use a portable generator, which can be expensive to run, or obtain mains electricity from a friendly source.

(2) Community halls

These can be particularly suitable if you are in a small town or village. Providing they are free for you to use these can be excellent bases for Christmas Cracker restaurants. The main drawback is that at Christmas they tend to be already in use a great deal.

(3) Large shops

It is sometimes worth approaching some of the large department stores or hypermarkets. Ask them if they have an on-site restaurant facility that they are not using. It could be one that is open to the public or a staff canteen. They may be willing to let you use it as it will attract customers to their store. If they do not have such a facility, you could suggest that for the three weeks they let you set one up in some part of the store.

(4) Church halls

These of course can be readily used. The disadvantage is that they are not a neutral venue like a high-street shop. However, if you use some imagination you could transform your church hall to look as much like a restaurant and as little like a church as possible. Whether you use your church will depend a great deal on where it is situated. There is no real point if it is a long way from the shopping centre.

6

Looking for Local Support

The Cracker Report

It's vital to keep the churches in your town well informed about your plans. When you register you will be sent a copy of some camera-ready artwork, just right for photocopying, along with a suggested design for a prayer and news sheet called 'The Cracker Report'. Use this to produce your own regular prayer letter which you can then distribute in your church and around the town.

Aim at getting the first issue out some time before the summer break and then follow it up with a new edition at the beginning of each month from September to December. December's copy should be fresh off the press just in time for the opening of your restaurant.

You might even decide to produce a final edition of 'The Cracker Report' for January to thank people for their support and give them news of the final figures raised as well as any encouraging news on the evangelistic front. The Cracker Report will serve as an information update to keep the project in the forefront of everybody's thinking, as well as giving important pointers for prayer and other forms of support and help. You'll discover that the artwork will also have many other uses as the months progress.

Decorating your restaurant

Nobody wants to eat in a shabby or unhygienic environment, so it's up to you and your group to make sure your Christmas Cracker is as clean, comfortable and well equipped as any other local restaurant. But the big question is, how do you achieve that without spending a fortune? There are all sorts of resources that you may be able to borrow free of charge or even be given. All you have to do is ask the right people.

Talk through the list of equipment and resources you need with your youth group. Find out whether they have any contacts who may be able to help provide what's needed. Maybe one of their dads, uncles or neighbours works in a local hardware store and will be able to persuade them to donate cans of paint, or maybe another runs a local shop which has some old unused cash registers out the back.

Ask your minister if you can have a spot in one of the Sunday services to talk briefly about the list of equipment needed. You never know what will turn up that way.

In your first Cracker Report print the list of equipment you need so that it gets circulated to all the churches in the town. Explain that all offers of help will be gratefully received. Make sure you put a contact phone number in.

What you need

To decorate your Christmas Cracker you will need:

* Paint
* Brushes/rollers etc
* Step-ladders
* Carpet
* Chairs
* Tables
* Lighting
* Plants

* Signwriting (on or above the front window)
* Street display boards

You will also need the following equipment:

* Cookers (find calor gas cookers if there is no gas supply to the premises)
* Cutlery
* Crockery
* Cooking utensils
* Fridge
* Freezer
* Two or three microwave ovens
* Two cash registers
* Heaters (electrical fan heating is convenient)
* Accounts books
* Washing-up liquid
* Tea towels
* Trays
* Serviettes
* Christmas Cracker T-shirts for staff

Sponsorship

A vital part of charity fundraising restaurants is sponsorship. The reason for this is simple. The more you have donated to you, by way of equipment and foodstuffs, the less you have to spend and the higher the profits that can go to relief and development.

It is no good going along and asking, 'Would you like to donate something?' Be specific; make a list of requirements.

Do not ask for everything from one supplier. For instance one supermarket could supply you tins of beans, while another supplies potatoes.

Be prepared to go back and ask a second time. Situations can change and persistence could pay dividends.

Be grateful for anything that you are given. Acknowledge the gift with a letter and by including your list of sponsors somewhere in your restaurant.

Your local high-street bank or building society may be able to give you a donation. Other businesses may do the same. Try to keep applications for help at a local level. Asking for help from head offices is rarely successful.

Why not get local businesses to sponsor the menus? They pay for one day's food supply, and the menu says, 'Today's menu sponsored by....'

Individuals could sponsor the cost of equipping one table.

Cut-price services are also a good form of sponsorship.

Finally, remember the following four points:

(1) Approach all your potential sponsors as early as possible. Don't leave everything to the last minute. It's up to you to inspire confidence by proving you are well organised and have realistically thought through your plans—nobody wants to support a flop!

(2) When you ask for sponsorship from big businesses with whom you don't have previous contact, it's helpful to present your ideas using attractive literature showing that you are part of a larger national project. Christmas Cracker provides a special eight-page Business Sponsor Brochure which has already been used nationally. It's well produced and gives a good introduction to what the Christmas Cracker is all about, as well as listing some of those companies who have already sponsored us.

(3) The Christmas Cracker office can also supply an attractive menu card which leaves plenty of room for details of your local dishes and lots of space for you to list the names of local sponsors. And there will obviously be lots of local press coverage as well as national media attention. Sponsorship equals good publicity.

(4) If a local business is part of a national chain it will not normally be possible for the manager to give you help without consulting head office.

7

What's on the Menu?

When your youth group sits down to plan your local menu, it is worth bearing one or two important principles in mind.

In 1983 when we ran the original 'Eat Less—Pay More' restaurant we started out by planning only to serve Third-World curries. We soon realised our mistake because we came across plenty of people who wanted to eat at the restaurant but weren't big fans of the local Indian take-away! As a result we broadened the menu out to include some simple English dishes. I recommend you do the same.

Your pre-printed menus will explain the 'pay as much as you like' principle (see below). You have to overprint them with the list of dishes you have available locally. Set a minimum price for each dish or drink. Customers can pay as much as they like but must meet your minimum price.

The restaurants are designed to give people a 'third-world experience' in terms of stimulating their thought about attitudes to wealth and helping provide them with an opportunity to contribute financially. They are not designed to give customers a bout of 'amoebic dysentry' as an aid to this process! The meals you serve must be hygienic and well prepared. Hygiene standards are dealt with in Chapter 10.

All the food served in your Christmas Cracker must be good quantity and quality. If a shopper pops in for lunch at your restaurant but is served with a meal which is neither appetising nor substantial enough to keep them going through the energy-draining business of afternoon Christmas shopping, you will not have done yourselves a service and they won't be coming back again. Remember a satisfied customer is your best advert!

Be practical—you're not the Ritz! Only choose items which are quick and easy to prepare. One of the reasons McDonald's is successful is because they stick to just a few items which are all simple to serve. Your menu must be designed with simplicity and efficiency in the kitchen in mind.

Sample menu

Soup	Mince Pies
Hamburger and Chips	Ice Cream
Chicken Nuggetts and Chips	Tea, Coffee, Coke,
Potatoes in their jackets	Orange Juice
Cheese on Toast	

Include recipes and other items which can be prepared at home by members of your youth group and other church members. For instance, the restaurant in Tonbridge always had a good supply of mince pies prepared in this way. All we had to do was warm them up in the microwaves and sell them.

A great deal of food you use in your restaurant will be donated by individuals and local businesses, but there are bound to be other items you need to buy.

Pricing policy

The underlying principle of Christmas Cracker is 'Eat less—pay more'. People will be served with simple meals and asked to donate a sum in excess of what they are likely to pay elsewhere. In 1989 some shops had their prices too low. Some were even undercutting other local eating establishments! It is important that the 'Eat less—pay more' principle is upheld. Prices do not have to be outrageous, but above what the customer could reasonably be expected to pay elsewhere.

This might sound like a recipe for disaster, but in the past restaurants with the highest prices have taken the most money. Such items as drinks and crisps can be sold at a reasonable price. On your menu give people guidelines on what they could donate. Have it printed clearly on the menu that these are not prices but *suggested minimum donations*. People are free to pay as much as they want.

Because the money that comes in is by donation only, people are entitled, if they so wish, to eat and then walk out without paying. This might seem ludicrous, but the donation principle is the most tax-effective way of raising funds.

Make giving lots of money fun. Display the highest price paid for a glass of water and encourage people to beat it.

Have a special highly priced dish of the day.

Put up all of your prices on one day and announce the upside down sale. 'Everything must go—all prices doubled!'

Allow groups to book for the evening. Serve a basic meal, and then get the tables to bid for such extras as:

* salt and pepper
* sauces or gravy
* a bottle of wine (we recommend non-alcoholic)
* after-dinner mints

* indeed anything that would add to the sparse meal that you have served them.

Merchandise

Besides good food it will be possible for your restaurant to stock both Christmas Cracker merchandise and Tearcraft products. Christmas Cracker merchandise includes badges, T-shirts, cards, balloons, posters and other items. A copy of the current year's Tearcraft catalogue and sales suggestions will be sent to you after registration.

Both Christmas Cracker and Tearcraft products make great Christmas presents, and in selling them you will increase the amount of aid sent to Christians working on relief and development projects in the Third World.

Attracting customers

Depending on your exact location, you may have to work very hard to let people know you are there. Distribute leaflets in the street. Get people out dressed as Christmas Crackers or clowns—and be *visible*.

Encourage local offices and businesses to come and have their Christmas meal there. It will certainly be a meal to remember.

Encourage church groups to book an evening at the restaurant.

If you live in an area where there are students or nurses, try to encourage them to come along. Christian Unions could use the restaurant for their Christmas outreach.

8

A Media-Friendly Cracker

by

Jenny Taylor

In 1989 newspapers, radio and TV stations up and down the country found lots to get their teeth into—and by Christmas the Cracker was national news.

A national media launch on London's South Bank was organised on September 25th, attended by various key figures from the Christian world, Ernie the National Champion Tug-of-War caller and 200 schoolchildren. This ensured that the project got off to a good start. We commissioned the construction of the world's largest ever Christmas cracker, to be pulled by the kids in front of witnesses for the Guinness Book of Records and marshalled by Big Ernie. BBC Newsround, Sky TV and Anglia TV were all there and we were broadcast across the nation, and Europe, that day.

There were national newspaper photographers, the Press Association, London radio reporters, the religious press and even the Government's Central Office of Information who were to inform all their embassies in Asia of this zany attempt to help the poor. The press were unsure at first, but the enthusiasm surrounding the whole project was infectious.

The nation's media were blanketed with a press release about the launch, using a national distribution agency. Then it was up to the groups. They kept their local media informed of progress, while we continued to work on the nationals. On Sunday December 17th teatime viewers of the BBC News witnessed Northampton's Cracker restaurant in business. Then, four days before Christmas, Radio 4's *Today* programme of news and current affairs (listened to, it is said, by Cabinet Ministers and even Mrs Thatcher) broadcast a feature taped at New Malden with Steve Chalke, and sounds of the group reaching its £5,000 target (entirely unscripted) in the background! On Christmas Eve itself, *The Mail on Sunday* ran a cheery piece entitled 'Cracking Cash-Raiser' above a story about how high interest rates were biting into the usual festive spending boom. Steve was quoted confidently denying this in our case: 'People will pay over the top when they know it's for a good cause,' he said.

It is notoriously difficult for a 'good news story', especially one connected with religion, to crack the secular media. Christmas Cracker, a good idea at the right time, did it with a combination of cheek and persistence — and an eye to playing the game by their rules.

We majored on picture stories and stunts. As Clifford Longley at *The Times* told me, newspapers are looking for more and more sophisticated gimmicks to capture the market. Robert Lustig wrote in *The Observer*'s 'This Week' column:

If a political diet fills you with gloom, take heart: imaginative gestures are alive and well. Tomorrow, a scheme to raise £1 million for the Third World will be launched at London's South Bank Centre. To pull the press, the organisers will pull the world's biggest Christmas cracker.

It worked!

We had already decided to offer prizes of free tickets to

India, courtesy of Air India, as incentive to groups to come up with their own publicity stunt. TVS covered Gravesend's attempt along the promenade to break the world conga record to launch their restaurant. The attempt failed, but the idea and the enthusiasm didn't. Anglia TV and Radio 4 covered the spectacular arrival with police motorcade of the fabled Prince of Biwani, alias Revah Khan, a local, and very game Asian squash player who opened their restaurant. And in Sutton Coldfield Radio WM did a live, and very entertaining roadshow from outside the Cracker where twenty-year-old Dean Phillips had locked himself into a freezing cage to draw attention to 'The Poverty Trap' and raise sponsorship. At Rayleigh they hired a bear from a visiting French circus to highlight the 'bear necessities' for survival in the Third World.

Publicity is a form of evangelism, allowing the light of the church to shine from its hill. We must learn to engage with the media, to command the agendas of our professional communicators by appropriate means. We must never let them off the hook!

Here are the publicity guidelines we gave the groups, which you can now follow too. All you have to do is appoint a Press and Publicity officer—and get cracking!

General considerations

Why tell the media? Because advertising is expensive, while a good story and picture are free! Christmas Cracker is a great story with which to grab the attention of non-churchgoers and get them curious enough to risk eating at your restaurant. Local news coverage gives great credibility to what you're doing.

Whom to contact

List all the newspapers, radio and TV stations that cover your area. There may be several that overlap. Don't forget the small, free papers. They are always looking for a good local picture story.

When you've done that, ring up and get the name of the youth editor. If there is no journalist with particular responsibility for youth, write to the News Editor. Some papers have a 'religious affairs correspondent'—but try to avoid getting consigned to the 'God spot'. You are not a minority interest!

Better still—does anyone in your congregation know any of the local reporters? Use your contacts. They will be grateful for a good story, and a personal contact will help guide you through the process sympathetically.

When and how to make contact

As soon as you've registered with Christmas Cracker, write a lively letter to the appropriate editor, telling him your plans and appealing for premises. It's a great way to get the paper (or radio station) involved and rooting for you at an early stage. Be sure to give a daytime and evening telephone number.

Once you've found premises, obtained planning permission and the show is definitely on the road, send in a lively letter giving them a 'date for the diary'—the opening date of your restaurant. Every newsdesk has its diary where events are logged weeks in advance.

A week or so later, ring up and ask to speak to the news editor. He or she will tell you what's happening about covering your event. Fix up to chat to the youth editor or whoever is appropriate to put them in the picture, and tell them what you've already done. A week before you officially open, ring up again and make sure everything's arranged for a reporter and a photographer to come. Occasionally, only a photographer covers picture stories, and will do a 'caption story'.

Once you've established a rapport, someone may want to take you on as a project, following your progress for a good feature item. It's worth a try, especially if you're a really big, dynamic group. If they don't take the bait, don't bludgeon them! No reporter wants to be made to feel duty-bound. Humour them, flatter them, take them for lunch, compliment their writing...but don't bully or nag. Better to wait until after the national launch.

What are they looking for?

In general, always work on the principle that what you don't tell reporters, they won't know.

The project

They will be particularly interested in where the money is going. Make sure you know! And make the most of this golden opportunity to bring the struggle of the Third World into the average UK living room.

Christmas Cracker has a lot of material on the projects supported, so try and avoid saying something vague about starvation or well-drilling. Read up on one or two projects that particularly appeal to you (these will be covered regularly in *21CC* magazine)—there are plenty of really imaginative, gripping things going on—and learn to summarise the information in a way that means something to a non-Christian stranger coming to the idea for the first time.

Newspapers and TV

Essentially, Christmas Cracker is a picture story. Think up some wacky visual stunt to launch your restaurant. You could have the youngest and oldest members of the congregation with paper hats on, pulling a giant Christmas cracker; teams from local schools pulling a giant cracker;

your youth leader carrying the mayor across the threshold
of the new restaurant; a dad in a chef's hat covered in
Christmas Cracker badges waving aloft a ladle and sam-
pling the first curry of the day from a giant cauldron. Make
up your mind what you're going to do, and go for it. The
photographer will handle the lighting problems and tell you
how they want to make the most of your idea. They may
want you to set it up specially to suit their deadlines, so find
out how you can help fit in with them. Remember: no
picture, no coverage.

Radio

Radio will want to pick up the atmosphere of the event
from sound. Singing children are irresistible (?!) on a radio
piece like this. A hilarious sketch? Something musical (but
go easy on the choruses!)? You could link up with your
local primary school, or your Sunday school.

The opening

Work out carefully what you most want to get across to the
public. Ask yourself what you're doing and why. Read up
on facts about the Third World from the Christmas Cracker
project pack; make it clear if you're from all sorts of different churches, and that you are supporting projects that
meet both physical and spiritual needs. Remember this is
an opportunity to start changing the way people think.

   Unless you've worked out what you want to say for
yourselves, you won't be able to articulate it when you're
on the spot. Practise on your mum! Or use someone who
has the gift of the gab in your youth group. *Don't use
jargon.* It's fine as shorthand for those in the know, but for
the average journalist it's an instant turn-off. Christmas
Cracker is all about relating faith to the everyday world,
not presenting ourselves as an exclusive club, so don't use
'kingdom-speak'.

All the people who've helped you should get an invitation to your opening: the estate agent who helped find the property and suppliers of equipment. They'll value the chance of being identified in the media with a good cause.

The opening is not just for the media—but to get the restaurant open for business, and to make friends. Warn the neighbours first. Explain to nearby cafés and restaurants that you are temporary, and charitable. Invite them round. They may feel you're threatening their trade, so they need to understand what you're about.

Run a competition

Can you get your local paper or commercial radio station to run a 'Facts about the Third World' competition promoting your restaurant, and offering as a prize a free meal there? Get the editor to award the prize at the opening. This roots your restaurant firmly in the local and international community and clearly demonstrates your concern, but you'll have to set it up carefully.

Follow-up

Once the restaurant is open, you will want to update the media on any big news that happens. Raised £5,000 in the first week? Let them know! Someone's donated an Elizabethan electric kettle? Let them know! You've had a million customers? (Keep a tally.) Let them know! Don't constantly bombard your pet reporter with data, but get back to him at least once a week after the opening—he'll be looking for good, Christmassy follow-up stories. Stick to the same reporter, otherwise you'll have to start all over again.

The Christmas Cracker office will be issuing national press releases on overall progress. If you are unable to answer any media question, refer them to the office. And remember to send the office copies of all press cuttings immediately you have them. These are crucial for generating national news and for their records.

9

Keeping the Accounts

Appointing a treasurer

The easy way

Simply pass the money raised as well as all invoices for expenditure relating to your restaurant straight to your church treasurer. Do this on a daily basis and let him do the hard work for you by handling the Christmas Cracker as a sub-division of the main church account.

The best way

In an earlier chapter I suggested that the position of the treasurer is one of the jobs that should be entrusted to a responsible member of the youth group. The person chosen doesn't necessarily need to be a trainee accountant or bank clerk, or even have a GCSE or A level in Maths. What is important is that they are totally honest, with a basic orderliness and understanding of numbers, old enough to open a bank account and enthusiastic in their approach.

Once appointed it's vital that you show confidence in the ability of the treasurer to be responsible for the job. Show interest and help out with problems without appearing to interfere.

Opening a bank account

Get the youth group member you appoint as Treasurer to shop around for an account. You want one where you don't pay bank charges when you're in credit, where the cheques are free and where a cheque card will immediately be issued.

The account should be opened in the name of 'The Christmas Cracker' followed by the name of your church and/or town, e.g. The Christmas Cracker—St Ebb's Margate. Set up the account to have three approved signatures and for each cheque to be signed by two out of these three. Because of the high-profile charity nature of the Cracker project it's very important that this kind of system—which ensures a high level of accountability—is established.

Ensure that all money is paid into the bank as soon as possible. Get your treasurer to talk with the church treasurer to get his help and advice. It may be helpful to open an account at the same bank as the main church account or existing youth group account.

Keeping a cash book

After each day's trading it's essential that the cash book is brought up to date. The cash book layout opposite has been chosen for simplicity and is what we would recommend. But if your treasurer has kept books before he may well have his own established system.

Invoices must be retained and numbered consecutively before being filed in order. Make a note of the cheque number and date of payment on each one. The number of the invoice should be entered in the cash book. There will be small essential items which need to be bought each day (like milk) where it is impractical to pay by cheque. The purchase of such items must be authorised by whoever is acting as shop manager at the time and bought from cash. The invoice must be entered into the till so that payment can be accounted for that evening. Cash should be banked once a day if possible.

CASH BOOK						
DATE	DETAILS	REF.	INCOME £ p	INVOICE NO.	EXP. £ p	BALANCE £ p
1989						
Nov 10	Balance	B/F	128.00			128.00
18	Gift	Cash	50.00			178.00
20	Cash & Carry Food	Cheque 001		001	38.40	139.60
27	Paint	Cheque 002		002	15.00	124.60
28	Tear Craft goods	Cheque 003		003	69.70	54.90
Dec 2	Restaurant—Food	Cash	153.35			208.25
	Tear Craft	Cash	45.80			254.05
	Tee Shirts	Cash	50.00			304.05
4	Restaurant—Food	Cash	90.25			394.30
	Tear Craft	Cash	12.50			406.80
	Tee Shirts	Cash	25.00			431.80
	Tea, Coffee, Milk etc	Cash		004-008	26.50	405.30
4	Balances		554.90		149.60	405.30

Insurance

The Christmas Cracker central office has negotiated an insurance policy to cover all restaurants registered in the scheme. The cover includes the breakage of plate-glass windows and even outbreaks of food-poisoning, as well as loss of funds on the premises or in transit. Each restaurant simply makes a small contribution towards the overall premium.

10

Health, Hygiene and Hotplates

Health regulations

In order to open as a restaurant you will need the permission of your local environmental health officer. You can contact him through the environmental health department of your local council. You will find him extremely helpful and only too willing to see your project succeed. Much of his advice will be sound common sense: keeping work surfaces clean and using the correct working practices with food. But codes regarding food hygiene are always under review, and local areas may have their own special regulations. The Officer will be able to provide you with helpful leaflets that you should read carefully and give to all those who will be taking part in the project. In some areas they may even be able to organise a training course for you.

Here are some general guidelines to be aware of from the outset:

(1) Keep all preparation, cooking and serving areas scrupulously clean and tidy. Be careful to clean areas where food might fall and go unnoticed—down the backs of cupboards, behind fridges etc.

(2) Keep floors tidy and wash them regularly.

(3) Make sure all cooking and eating utensils are clean. Remember that just because they come out of a cutlery drawer, that doesn't mean they are clean. Check before you use them.

(4) Take extra care with regard to storing food. Different foods require different storage conditions. You must take care that food is stored at the correct temperature, and that one item cannot interfere with another. This is particularly important with liquids that may drip from one container to another. Raw food should be stored and handled separately from cooked food—this is especially important where poultry is involved. Stored food should be used before moving on to more recently acquired food.

(5) All those who work in the restaurant should be clean and tidy with hands washed regularly. Make sure there are ample supplies of soap; clean, dry towels; clean aprons or overalls; plasters and other items of first aid. Instruct workers to keep fingernails short, to avoid nail varnish and finger jewellery, to refrain from smoking, and to inform you immediately if they are feeling unwell. Someone coughing and sneezing is an obvious health hazard—as well as a deterrent to customers!

(6) Discourage customers from smoking, unless you have room for a separate area, and from bringing animals onto the premises.

You should write a letter to your local Environmental Health Officer as early as possible. Don't wait until you've finalised the availability of a shop, write to let him know who you are and what Christmas Cracker is all about as early as possible. After you have registered with Christmas

Cracker you will receive a draft letter which you can use as a guide.

Wait two weeks and then follow up your letter with a phone call. Arrange an appointment to chat things over.

Registration with Christmas Cracker also means you receive simple guidelines on hygiene to ensure that your restaurant's standards are in line with British Health and Safety regulations, plus a list of official publications which cover the use of frozen foods, cooking with boiled and fried rice, using microwave ovens, safety with electricity, personal hygiene and the general ten-point code for workers in the food trade. When you book to meet your Environmental Health Officer make sure you take them along to show him that you've already taken the whole subject seriously enough to get yourself well informed.

If the shop you finally obtain was not previously used to serve and sell food you will also need to contact the Planning Officer (another Local Authority employee) and obtain a licence for temporary change. Our office has already published a letter in *Planning*, the official magazine for planning officers, informing them about Christmas Cracker and asking for their help. Our advice is that you should now get in touch with your local officer as soon as possible so that if you do eventually find yourself needing his help you've already established a relationship. Once again, a draft letter is available for this purpose. Even the kind of temporary licence you need can be very difficult to obtain without the help of a sympathetic officer.

Both your Environmental Health and Planning Officer are employees of the Local Authority. You can obtain their names, business addresses and phone numbers by ringing your local town hall.

Fire regulations

Once again, although this is an essential area to sort out, it's not the minefield that you might at first imagine.

Write to the Chief Officer at your local fire station. Explain what the Christmas Cracker project is all about and ask for his advice and help once you've got your shop. Once again, the Christmas Cracker registration pack includes a draft letter for this purpose. Remember: early contact always helps.

Once you have a shop ask for a visit from the fire brigade to talk through safety precautions. Show that you are aware of the relevant issues by taking the initiative to raise them with the officers who visit you. Ask about:

* Escape routes from the premises in case of fire.

* Emergency lighting and fire-exit signs.

* Procedure in the event of a fire.

* The contents of a simple fire-instruction notice.

* The number and type of fire extinguishers needed (you can then approach a local fire security firm for the free loan of these over the Christmas period).

* The safe use of any flammable liquids and naked flames.

* The maximum number of customers who should be allowed on the premises at any one time.

The central insurance policy covers any injury from fire to staff or customers. The building itself will be insured by its owner. Ask the estate agent you deal with to check this.

Gas and electricity

In many cases it's probably easier to opt for using only electricity, though if there's an existing gas supply which terminates at a suitable point it may make sense to use this as well. When we ran the first restaurant in Tonbridge six years ago we used two small Calor gas stoves but did the vast majority of our cooking in three microwave ovens which a catering company loaned to us free of charge.

Once you've got your shop, contact your local gas and/or electricity showroom and ask for the supply to be reconnected. The electricity should be connected at least a week before the restaurant opens because you need power to start kitting out and decorating it before the opening day.

Explain that you only want the supply until the end of the project and that you require a final bill as soon as possible after that date. Ask them if they will supply free or at a special rate. In 1989 several of the restaurants benefited from the generosity of local electricity and gas boards.

Having received your bill(s) all you have to do is deduct that amount from the final total you'll be sending in to the Christmas Cracker fund. Make sure to show this clearly in your accounts and keep evidence of payment.

11

Unwrapping Christmas

The Cracker table card

The central office has produced a special table card for use
in the restaurants, featuring the Christmas Cracker logo on
the front. It opens up to explain why the restaurants are
being run and what Christmas is really all about. It ends by
suggesting that if the reader is interested in knowing more
they should chat to a member of the staff or fill in the cut-
off slip and post it to the address given. (The card allows
space for you to overprint a local address.) It also mentions
that there are local Christmas carol services planned to
which the reader is welcome and states that details are to be
found on the back cover (once again space is left for over-
printing).

So what do you do if a customer wants to know more
about the real meaning of Christmas and what a Christian
is? Your youth group must be prepared.

How to prepare and use a personal testimony

The term 'testimony' tends to put people off but actually simply relates to using your personal story to explain what a Christian is in a clear way. Effectively communicating to other people why you became a Christian is a real art, but it can be one of the most powerful tools for presenting the gospel in a brief and interesting way. It requires thorough preparation because the better prepared the testimony, the more naturally it will be presented.

Get each member of your group to sit down with a sheet of A4 paper and a pen. Ask them to write down the following three headings, with space below each.

* Before I received Christ.

* How I received Christ—what happened.

* After I received Christ—what has changed.

Now get them to put down short relevant phrases under each of these headings. Give them five minutes to do this and then ask them to write up complete sentences to expand the phrases.

Explain that the rules for doing this are:

(1) Be simple. Don't use spiritual jargon like 'saved', 'convicted', 'born again'.

(2) Be specific. Mention real details, like a place you went to, a person you talked with, attitudes you had, what you prayed when you became a Christian.

(3) Be honest. Don't exaggerate. Believe it or not, it's not true that the most powerful testimony is necessarily the one with the most sex, drugs and violence in it.

(4) Don't try to paint a perfect picture. Again this is about honesty. Jesus Christ didn't promise life without prob-

lems but simply the peace and confidence to cope with
the reality of day-to-day living. Don't try to deceive
people into believing in something you personally have
not discovered.

Next get your group into threes to present their testi-
monies to each other and to make honest comments about
what is said. Get each young person to record the relevant
comments that the others make.

Send the youth group members home with their sheets of
paper to work through more exactly what they are going to
say. Suggest that they read aloud to themselves what they
have written and re-write it two or three times until they are
happy with the way it flows. Now it's up to them to learn by
heart what they've written out. This should not be done in a
mechanical fashion but simply to the point where they have
a good grasp of the subject matter they want to cover. Now
when the opportunity arises they will be able to talk in a
relaxed, natural and informative way about how they
became a Christian and why.

Using an evangelistic booklet

Make sure you get a good stock of an evangelistic booklet
which presents the gospel in a clear and relevant way. We
recommend:

* *Christmas Unwrapped* (by Steve Chalke)

* *Journey into Life* (not the cheapest but unbeatable).

* *How to Know God Personally* (clear and cheap).

* *Bridge to Life* (also budget-priced).

There are of course many other simple but effective
booklets of this nature available from your local Christian
bookshop. Do not raid a dusty cupboard in your church

where copies of old tracts have been gently going mouldy. Use one attractive, up-to-date title rather than a collection of odds and ends. Book a session with your youth group one or two weeks before the restaurant is due to open to run through the outline of your chosen booklet. If you've never studied how to present the gospel to a non-Christian, get hold of the booklet *Tell What God Has Done* (published by the Bible Society) or an equivalent suggested by your local Christian bookshop, and work through it carefully before instructing your young people. Here are some basic principles you may find helpful.

(1) If you are in a conversation where somebody wants to know more about what a Christian is, explain that you have a booklet on display in the shop which they might find helpful to look at. Get up, collect a copy and sit back down with them.

(2) Hold the booklet so that you can both see it and point to the words and sentences as you read them.

(3) Read the booklet aloud but not mechanically. Pause to explain more fully the points the booklet makes.

(4) Give the person you are talking to plenty of opportunity to ask questions. You can do this by asking questions like 'Does this make sense?' or 'Do you understand that?'

(5) If the person has a lot of questions which are off the point, a helpful way to keep them on track is to respond with a comment like: 'That's a good question, we could talk about it after we've finished going through the booklet.' Often questions asked will be answered by the rest of the booklet, but if that's not the case then you can chat over any other points after you've been able clearly to present the principles of becoming a Christian. Whenever possible maintain the direction of

thought which the booklet outlines. This enables you to avoid the problem of ending up talking round and round in circles and never getting anywhere.

(6) Never force or push a customer to talk. Always be polite, whatever response you get. *The majority of people who eat at your restaurant will probably not enter into conversation about Christian things. Never try to manipulate the situation, leave them alone to enjoy their meal.* But remember, just because they don't talk doesn't mean they are not impressed and challenged by your project. Maybe some of them will fill in the table card and send it back to you or attend a local carol service.

Remember, some people have come simply to eat and donate money and it is neither courteous nor worth losing their return custom by forcing your views on them. A Christmas Cracker with a name for being a Bible-bashing shop will soon also have one for being empty!

PART TWO

Christmas Cracker—Here's Why

Leaders' Guide

One of the real difficulties in preparing studies for youth groups is quite simply that they are all different. They are different not only in size and average age but in the amount of time they spend together and the depth to which they want to study.

The aim of these study outlines is to give you, the leader, flexibility. You will notice that each outline includes several elements. There are the Bible studies themselves, along with crowdbreakers and group activities. There is also a section at the back of this book (Chapter 12) with additional general material and games which you may choose to use as you feel they are appropriate to your group. Basically you should use each study as your base and then build the other material around it as time permits. Once your youth group has discovered the why you can begin to earth what you've learnt by working on the project material.

Whatever you do, please don't feel that you have to cram every single part of the material into your evening. Examine the material and decide which will work best for your group. You may well decide that you want to cover one subject over two evenings. One evening where you examine the Bible study material, and another evening where you look at the project material and some of the practical implications of the Bible study.

The audio-visual guide at the end of this book will help you see what other resources are available to your group on the subject of mission. You may wish to include them alongside your Bible studies, or you may wish to use them on a separate occasion to follow up what you've learnt.

Planning

Here are a few tips to help you with your planning.

Read the notes carefully

Make sure that the first time you read the material it is not at your youth group's meeting! Work through the material on your own.

Materials

Make sure that there is enough material for everybody. In Chapter 11 we've given guidelines on how to produce worksheets for the prayer concert.

Have your resources ready

Make sure that you have a good supply of pens and paper. It's also a good idea to have a few spare copies of the Bible around. Not everyone possesses a Bible and even those who do don't always bring it along to the youth group. If you are planning to use an overhead projector, make sure that you have pens and acetates ready for use.

Videos

If you intend showing a video on a particular evening, make sure that you order it well in advance. And remember to ensure beforehand that the video and television that you are using are in good working order.

Involvement

It's good to get your youth group involved, whether it's in taking prayers, leading worship or doing a reading. But don't expect them to do something well at five minutes' notice—they need advance warning. Make sure the musicians know well in advance which songs you are going to sing, and that all others taking part are well briefed. This is particularly important if you are going to need leaders of small groups for prayer or Bible study.

It sounds like an awful lot of work, but a little advanced planning will make things run more smoothly on the night. Prepare well and surround the evening with prayer.

On the night

On the night, begin with worship. The exact form and content of the worship will depend on your group. Worship is important as it sets the Bible studies in context and makes us aware of God's presence with us. As you worship pray that the Holy Spirit will open your eyes and hearts as you study his word.

You will notice that the Bible studies consist largely of reading the passage and answering some fairly simple questions. Be imaginative with this. If your group is large, split up into smaller groups and encourage the groups to feed back to you. Some of the questions have fairly straightforward answers, but don't be afraid to ask the group how they actually feel about the issues raised.

At the same time as allowing freedom of discussion, don't let things get carried away! It is very easy for a group to go off at tangents into unrelated subjects, and to lose track of the aim of the evening. Encourage the group to pray about what they've learnt, and to think about ways in which they can respond to what they've heard from the Bible.

The aim of it all

The aim of the project material is to inform you and your group of the needs of the world and how God's people are meeting those needs. If your church has links with missionaries overseas then use their prayer and newsletters.

Be prepared to share with the leadership of your church what you are doing. Make sure your pastor or elder sees a copy of this book. Ask the leadership of your church if the youth group can share in Sunday services. Ask some of the group to write down what they are learning and perhaps have this published in your monthly church magazine. Above all, show your church that the youth group is interested in mission. This will give the young people an obvious outlet for what they have learnt. It should also greatly encourage the whole church and inspire them to think seriously about mission.

Above all, surround all that you do with prayer. Expect God to work in the lives of the young people. Expect him to call some of them to full-time missionary service. Expect him to speak to them as they are challenged about their lifestyle and what they are doing for him.

1

What Kind of God Is He?

For leaders

Read John 1:1–14.

Aim: To show that God is an outgoing, missionary God.

Starting off

What is God like?

Play the *What Kind Of?* game described under the *Crowdbreaker* heading. Although this will provoke hilarity, it does have a serious side. The purpose of the game is to try to draw out some of the characteristics of God. This will help the group to discover the views they hold about God. As they complete the questions, ask them to give reasons for their choices, and ask others to comment, either for or against. For example, could God be a Rolls Royce, because of its superiority and reliability? You need to use your imagination for this game.

Owner's manual

This passage from John's Gospel is commonly known as the prologue. It is different from the beginning of the other

Gospels. Matthew and Luke both begin with historical accounts of the birth of Jesus, while Mark launches straight into the ministry of Jesus. John, however, deals with Jesus' existence before time, and how the eternal God broke into history. In describing Jesus, John uses the expression 'The Word of God'.

John wanted to use an expression that would be known to both his Jewish and Greek readers, so he chose the expression 'the Word'. To the Greeks, the Word was the force that held everything together, a cosmic power that gave order to the universe. The Jews felt that the word 'God' was too sacred for them to say, so they used other words like 'Lord', and by John's time they also used 'Word'. So to the Jews, 'the Word' was an expression for God.

For group members

Crowdbreaker

We all have different characteristics. Sometimes we can liken these characteristics to familiar objects: 'sweet as sugar', or 'hard as nails'. Think about God and answer the questions below, giving reasons for your choices.

If God was a car, what kind would he be? If God were a rescue service, which one would he be? If God were an article of clothing, what kind would it be? If God were a famous person, who would he be? If God were a food or drink, what would it be?

Bible study

Read Genesis 1:3, 6, 9. What happened when God spoke?

Now look at Isaiah 55:10–11. Think about the effectiveness of these facts (v 10). How then does v 11 affect your view of what God can do?

Read John 1:1–14. Where was the Word in the beginning? (v 1)

What does this tell us about the Word? (v 1)
List what the Word has done. (v 3, 10)
What does this tell us about God? (v 14)

Real life

You are walking by a lake when you see someone apparently in trouble in the water. You realise that you have to do something. There is a rope nearby, as well as a life jacket. You are also a good swimmer. You quickly assess the situation. The options open to you are:

1. Throw the person the rope.

2. Throw the life jacket.

3. Dive in and rescue him.

4. Shout, 'I love you, I'm sure you'll be all right!'

Think about the pros and cons for each of the actions.
  'The Word became flesh' (John 1:14). Which of the above is nearest to the action described in the verse?

2

What Kind of People Should We Be?

For leaders

Read 1 Peter 2:4–12.

Aim: To answer the question, 'Is mission an optional extra?'

Starting off

Get the group to complete the *True or False?* checklist. Follow this with a brief time of discussion on each of the questions. This will help to reveal the attitudes of the group towards the church.

Owner's manual

With all the activities that we run and meetings we attend, it would be easy to come to the conclusion that the church exists primarily for itself and that reaching out to people is something of an optional extra. Biblically speaking, nothing could be further from the truth. The passage from 1 Peter begins with the formation of a people and moves on to the purpose of that people—to reach out to the world, to declare the praises of God. Acts Chapter 2 clearly shows that the church's birthright was in mission. Jesus' commission to the disciples shows this too (Matthew 28:19; John 20:21). In the New Testament letters, where internal church matters are dealt with, the aim of the writers was to help the churches to become more effective in their ministry. Even instruction on pastoral care and loving one another is given so that the world will know that we are disciples of Christ.

This section includes *A Fishy Parable*. This can be useful in exploring some of the reasons why we, the church, don't get involved in effective mission.

For group members

Crowdbreaker

The *True or False?* checklist...

1. Churches were started by the early Christians to keep Christianity alive.

2. Churches should be made up of people trying to find God.

3. Not every 'church' on the corner of the street is what Jesus would call a church.

4. The priority of a church should be to provide a good social atmosphere in the community.

5. By your understanding of the New Testament, your youth fellowship could be called a church.

6. The church building has very little to do with the real church.

7. A Christian can accomplish what a church does, simply by being alone with the Lord.

Bible study

Read Matthew 16:18. Who started the church and who is going to stop it?

Read 1 Peter 2:4–12. Who is *the* living stone? (v 4)

What are we being built into? (v 5)

Look at Acts 2:24–47. What church activities were the early Christians regularly involved in?

God has called us together for what purpose? *1 Peter 2:9.*

Look at Ephesians 4:11–12. What is the purpose of the ministries that God has given to the church?

What do you think 'works of service' means for your fellowship?

What is the state of the world, according to Paul? *Romans 1:18–25.*

Read Matthew 28:19. How important do you think this statement is? Do you think Jesus meant this as an optional extra?

Read Romans 10:14–15. Is there any way that people will hear the message without the church going to them?

A FISHY PARABLE

'For months the Fishers' Society had been wracked with dissension. They had built a new meeting hall which they called their Aquarium and had even called a world-renowned Fisherman's Manual scholar to lecture them on the art of fishing. But still no fish were caught.

Several times each week they would gather in their ornate Aquarium Hall, recite portions of the Fisherman's Manual and then listen to their scholar expound the intricacies and mysteries of the Manual. The meeting would usually end with the scholar dramatically casting his net into the large tank in the centre of the hall and the members rushing excitedly to its edges to see if any fish would bite. None ever did of course, since there were not any fish in the tank.

Which brings us to the reason for the controversy. Why? The temperature of the tank was carefully regulated to be just right for ocean perch. Indeed, oceanography experts had been consulted to make the environment of the tank nearly indistinguishable from the ocean. But still no fish. Some blamed it on poor attendance at the society's meetings. Others were convinced that specialisation was the answer: perhaps several small tanks geared especially for different fish age-groups.

There was even a division over which was more important: casting or providing optimum tank conditions.

Eventually a solution was reached. A few members of the society were commissioned to become professional fishermen and were sent to live a few blocks away on the edge of the sea and do nothing but catch fish.

It was a lonely existence because most other members of the society were terrified of the ocean. So the professionals would send back pictures of themselves holding some of their catches and letters describing the joys and tribulations of real, live fishing.

And periodically they would return to Aquarium Hall to show slides. After such meetings, people of the society would return to their homes thankful that their hall had not been built in vain.'

Reprinted from the Wittenburg Door.

This is a parable, but how does it reflect the situations that we find in the church today?

3

What Is World Mission?

For leaders

Read Luke 4:14–21.

Aim: to understand the breadth of the gospel.

Starting off

Get the group to do the *Essential Pursuit* quiz on world mission.

The answers are: 1 b, 2 c, 3 d, 4 c, 5 b, 6 c, 7 b, 8 c, 9 b, 10 a, 11 d, 12 c, 13 a, 14 b, 15 d, 16 a, 17 b, 18 d, 19 b, 20 b.

The purpose of the quiz is to show the extent of world need and therefore set the background to the Bible study on the breadth of the gospel.

Owner's manual

Mission is not an easy concept to tie down. To some it simply means 'preaching the gospel', to others it is 'social action' or a combination of the two. As you look through the Bible you will see that God is concerned about social injustice, but that the root cause of that is human rebellion against God. So when Jesus came, he came to die for our sins, but he was also forthright in his condemnation of social injustice. He taught that what comes out of a man, in words and actions, comes from inside, from a heart that is hardened to God (see Luke 6:45). It is important that we show care to people because Christ cared for those in need. We also need to recognise that injustice and poverty are symptoms of our rebellion against God and that we must deal with the root cause—sin.

If mission has this breadth, then there is a whole host of ways in which we can become involved.

For group members

ESSENTIAL PURSUIT

1. What is the present world population to the nearest billion (thousand million)?

a) 3 billion
b) 5 billion
c) 8 billion
d) 11 billion

2. How many children die each year in third world countries from dehydration caused by diarrhoea?

a) 500
b) 3,000
c) 7,000
d) 38,000

3. The total number of child deaths in the third world each day is:

a) 19,000
b) 16,000
c) 25,000
d) 38,000

4. The amount of water used every day by each person in Britain is about:

a) *10 gallons*
b) *15 gallons*
c) *40 gallons*
d) *55 gallons*

5. In rural areas of the third world people with clean water number:

a) *20 per cent*
b) *30 per cent*
c) *40 per cent*
d) *50 per cent*

6. What percentage of all diseases is caused by polluted water?

a) *60 per cent*
b) *70 per cent*
c) *80 per cent*
d) *90 per cent*

7. How many times has Bangladesh been flooded in the past thirty years?

a) *5*
b) *13*
c) *16*
d) *19*

8. Bangladesh has a population of 110 million. After the floods of 1988, how many of these were estimated to be homeless?

a) *12 million*
b) *27 million*
c) *48 million*

d) 61 million

9. At the height of the 1988 flood the streets of Dhaka were swirling with raw sewage. How many gallons of sewage were emptying into the streets each day?

a) 3 million
b) 40 million
c) 50 million
d) 55 million

10. How much of the world's population could be described as poor?

a) Three-quarters
b) One-quarter
c) Half
d) One-third

11. How much of the world's wealth is consumed by the Western world?

a) Half
b) One-quarter
c) Two-thirds
d) Three-quarters

12. The average family in Western Europe spends between 25 and 30 per cent of their income on food. What percentage does a third-world family spend in this way?

a) 40–50 per cent
b) 55–65 per cent
c) 80–90 per cent
d) 90–95 per cent

13. In Britain there is one doctor (including specialists) for about every:

a) 650 people
b) 950 people
c) 1,300 people
d) 1,500 people

14. In Nepal there is one doctor for about every:

a) 40,000 people
b) 30,000 people
c) 10,000 people
d) 5,000 people

15. There are about 86 million evangelical Christians in Western and Eastern Europe. How many are there estimated to be in the third world?

a) 55 million
b) 74 million
c) 102 million
d) 174 million

16. In Africa 25 per cent of the population go to church regularly. In Great Britain the percentage is:

a) 5 per cent
b) 7 per cent
c) 10 per cent
d) 12 per cent

17. Worldwide, how many people become Christians daily?

a) 17,000
b) 63,000
c) 112,000
d) 175,000

18. How many new churches are established worldwide each week?

a) *100*
b) *800*
c) *1,200*
d) *1,600*

19. How many people in the world have never been evangelised (to the nearest billion)?

a) *1 billion*
b) *2 billion*
c) *4 billion*
d) *5 billion*

20. There are approximately 12,000 different languages used around the world. How many of these are still without any Christian witness?

a) *1,000*
b) *4,000*
c) *6,000*
d) *7,000*

Bible study

Read Amos 2:6–16.

Of what is Israel accused? (v 6–10)
Israel really had no excuse for behaving like this because:
God had saved them (v 10): 'I brought you out of Egypt.'
God had protected them (v 9): 'I destroyed the Amonites.'
Why do you think they behaved the way they did?
Read Isaiah 53:6a. What is the root cause of such behaviour?
What is the remedy? Look at Amos 5:14–15.
Read Mark 1:14–15. The kingdom of God is God's rule. What Jesus was saying was that the time of God's rule was

at hand. With the inbreaking of the kingdom, Jesus announces that there is an appropriate action to accompany it. What is that action?

When Jesus went to the synagogue and read, he read from the Old Testament (Isaiah 61:1–2) and he said that this prophecy was fulfilled in his coming.

Do you think Jesus was only concerned with spiritual matters?

Why did you answer the way you did?

When you became a Christian, you not only received a new identity as a child of God but you also received a new wardrobe.

Look at Colossians Chapter 3.

What are we to take off? (v 5–9)

What are we to replace it with? (v 10, 12–14) How do you think your faith should affect the world?

Look at Matthew 28:19.

What things did Jesus ask his disciples to do?

In what practical ways could you serve the kingdom of God? Look up Romans 12:6–8. You'll see that it is not only preachers and teachers, but all kinds of people with all kinds of gifts who can be involved. The question is not 'what is there to do?' but 'what is God calling me to do?'

Real-life situation

Try finishing your session by looking at the following problem:

Imagine you are the creative genius in an advertising agency. A leading politician has come up with a plan for solving the world's problems. He asks you to devise a campaign to sell it to the rich, the poor and the plain uninterested. What ideas would you come up with to persuade people that this man could meet their needs? What would you emphasise?

4

What Can I Do?

For leaders

Read Luke 5:1–11; 27–32.

Aim: To look at the sort of people Jesus calls to serve him.

Starting off

You will need pins, pens and paper. Get each of the group to pin a sheet of paper to someone else's back. They should now go around the room and write on each person's piece of paper a compliment (nice dress or great shoes) or, if they know them a little better, one of their qualities. Let this run for a few minutes. Then ask everyone to pair off and read each other's lists.

Owner's manual

Most of us make excuses as to why we can't be involved in mission. 'I don't know any non-Christians' or 'I'm too busy', or 'I'm not the right kind of person', or 'God doesn't use people like me'. Just about every Christian at one time or another has made an excuse. Peter and his friends probably felt more comfortable catching fish or counting money than being evangelists, but Jesus took them and used them for his purposes. This study looks at Jesus' first disciples. It shows that God calls people that the world might consider unsuitable.

'Dear children, let us not love with words or tongue but with actions.' *1 John 3:18*

For group members

Bible study

Begin by reading Judges 6:1–16.

1. What were the sort of problems that faced the people of Israel?

2. What was Gideon's assessment of his own ability?

3. What was God's assessment of Gideon's ability?

Now look at Luke 5:1–11; 27–32.

1. What were the fishermen doing when Jesus and the crowd arrived (vv 1–2)? Why didn't Peter notice Jesus' need for help?

2. Why was Peter reluctant to comply with Jesus' request?

3. What do you think Peter and Matthew were good at? What do you think they were bad at?

4. Why does this event cause such strong reactions in Peter and his companions? (vv 6–10)

What gifts do you think you have?

What reasons would God give not to use you? *Look at 1 Corinthians 1:27–29.*

Do the first disciples fit into this description? Do you?

Real-life situation

Your church has asked you to compile a job description for a vacancy in one of its organisations. Bearing in mind that they may have all the professional qualifications, what kind of character qualities would you look for in them? How do these match up to a description you might make of Peter?

5

What Do Missionaries Do?

For leaders

Read Luke 10:1–9, 25–37.

Aim: To answer the question, 'Do we feed the hungry or preach to them?'

Starting off

Start by asking the group to complete the *Missionary Disinformation* questionnaire. This is to bring into the open some of the most common preconceptions about missionaries and mission. After this, move on to the discussion starters.

Owner's manual

In Study 3 we examined the breadth of human need and the breadth of Jesus' mission. In Study 2 we saw that being a witness was the responsibility of every Christian and that mission was the bread-and-butter activity of the church. The question now is: what is our priority, to preach or to care?

Christians have tied themselves in knots over this issue

and become (tragically) polarised. An interesting note from Luke 10 is that the sending out of the seventy-two is followed by the parable of the Good Samaritan.

In the life and ministry of Jesus we see preaching accompanying acts of mercy. Matthew's Gospel describes an incident in which Jesus uses not only words but actions. The outcome points to Jesus' true nature as genuine love made visible (see Matthew 11:2–5).

Jesus wanted to emphasise that loving God and loving people cannot be separated, and that loving means action. If we truly love people, we will want to care for them. If we truly care for them, we will be concerned with their eternal state, their relationship with God. A famous preacher called Charles Spurgeon once said, 'If you're going to give a hungry man a tract, make sure you wrap it in some bread.'

Practically, one aspect usually takes precedence over the other, depending on the circumstances. But both caring and preaching depend on each other.

The *Real-Life Situations* try to earth the Bible study in some concrete circumstances. Divide the group into two and get each group to consider one of the situations. The second situation is real. World Vision were asked to help and they placed a Christian couple in the village (David and Tiptri) to help advise on health and hygiene and to provide a Christian witness. It was through their love and practical concern that interest was generated in Christ.

For group members

Crowdbreaker

Missionary Disinformation: Write the word 'true' or 'false' against each statement. To be a missionary:

    You need to be spiritual
    You have to like spiders
    You must speak other languages
    You can be an office clerk or mechanic

You must not get married
You must hate leaving Britain
You must be able to speak publicly
You must live on very little

Discussion starter

1. Missionary work today is about health projects and helping the poor—not about preaching the gospel. Is this true?

2. What do you think are the most important qualities for a missionary to have and why?

Read Luke 10:1–9.

What is the harvest that Jesus refers to? (v 2)

What, in practical terms, would it mean for the seventy-two to be sheep among wolves?

What would it mean for you?

Look at Luke 9:2—the sending out of the twelve.

What did Jesus tell them to do?

Now read Luke 10:25–37.

To whom is love to be directed? (v 27)

Try to show this relationship in a diagram.

What does this say about our relationship with God and the people around us?

Do you think that the expert wanted to get out of his responsibility? Why?

In what ways did it cost the Samaritan to show care?

Do you think Luke 9:2 and Luke 10:25–37 are contradictory? Give the reasons for your answer.

If you have time, read through Mark Chapters 1–3. Look at the way in which preaching the gospel and showing care exist side by side. Too often we create separation where Jesus never did. Sometimes preaching took priority over care, and sometimes things happened the other way round.

Real-life situations

1. Lyn is a single parent who lives alone with her small child. The conditions she lives in are appalling. She has very little money and finds it difficult to make ends meet. She is not a Christian, but has contact with your church through a mother-and-toddler club. You are in regular contact with her. You know her financial needs, and you also know that she needs Christ. What are your priorities? What do you deal with first, her physical situation or her spiritual condition? Give reasons for your answers.

2. Chapeldandi is a small fishing village in the south-east corner of Bangladesh, not far from the Burmese border. The people of the village earn their living from fishing and making cloth. The village is a mix of Muslims, Hindus and Buddhists. There are no Christians in the village. The water supply in the village is poor; the source is a stagnant pool used for washing, drinking and as a public toilet. Health care is very low, with a high incidence of childhood illnesses such as measles, leading to death. Due to the poor water supply and bad diet, diseases relating to diarrhoea are high. Education is basic, with very few people being able to read. They scrape a living, mainly because they have to sell to middle men and not directly to their customers.

The people of Chapeldandi approach your Christian organisation and ask for help. You decide to draw up a five-year programme. In view of their needs, what would be your priorities? What kind of personnel would you bring in to help the villagers? What goals would you have for each year of the programme?

6

The Reality of Mission

For leaders

Read Luke 8:1–15 (and Mark 4:1).

Aim: To understand the realities of mission and evangelism worldwide.

Starting off

Play the communications game below. This will emphasise the difficulties of communication and the point that what is sent is not always received, or received in the correct form.

Arrange players into couples, with each of the partners at opposite sides of the room. Use all the walls so that the players are spaced around the hall. One member of each couple (the boss) is given a prepared newspaper cutting (use six different messages of approximately the same length), while the other member (secretary) has a piece of paper and a pencil. On the signal to start, the bosses begin dictating the contents of the newspaper cutting to the secretaries who try to take it down. This is a difficult task with so many competing voices. The first couple with a complete, correct message of dictation are the winners.

Variation: to make it more difficult, have the bosses sucking a sweet, standing on a chair on one leg.

Owner's manual

It is right that we should be positive in our approach to mission and evangelism—the gospel is the power of salvation (Romans 1:16). However, we must be realistic. Firstly, we are involved in spiritual warfare; and secondly, Jesus warned us that there would be those who would try to take an easier route—which only led to destruction (Matthew 7:13). This study explains what the Bible says about the reasons why people reject the gospel. In the *Real-Life Situations* section, you will look at the world and see the extent of the need. But don't leave your group feeling totally discouraged. Emphasise the power of Jesus Christ and his ultimate victory (Philippians 2:11).

For group members

Crowdbreaker

Find yourself a partner and then follow the instructions of your leader.

   Read Luke 8:1–15.

Identify the different types of soil in the parable and match them below with the different types of hearers.

   Miss Apathetic
   Mrs Superficial
   Mr Preoccupied
   Mr Goodsoil

What kind of people would these people be and what would be their characteristics?

   Apathetic Hearer
   Superficial Hearer
   Preoccupied Hearer
   Good Hearer

Now read Ephesians 6:10–12. Is our battle merely restricted to what we can see and observe?

Read 2 Corinthians 4:4. Who is it that has blinded people to the truth?

Is it realistic to expect everybody to become Christians? Look at Matthew 7:13.

How does this make you feel?

Discouraged
Annoyed
Encouraged
Couldn't care less

2 Timothy 4:4. This verse tells us that people will 'turn their ears away from the truth and turn aside to myths'. What evidence is there that people are doing this today?

Acts 7:11. Why could the Bereans be classed as good hearers?

Philippians 2:9. Who is going to have the victory in the end?

Romans 1:16. 'I am not ashamed of the gospel, because it is the power of God for the salvation of everyone who believes.'

Real-life situations

Why bother about the rest of the world? Surely everyone has heard of Christ by now? Many people believe that everyone in the world has heard of Jesus, but the reality is very different. Although the church is growing worldwide, and in some parts of the world is even outstripping the birth rate, nevertheless there are many people-groups still totally unreached. The facts below show the extent of the need.

Over 4.5 billion people need Christ as Lord and Saviour.

Millions are unreached on new frontiers and in great growing cities.

The billion people in Chinese, Muslim, Hindu and Buddhist cultures need the gospel.

Among the more than one billion called Christian

(whether Protestant, Orthodox or Catholic), millions have not trusted in Christ personally.

Most nominal Christians know Christ died on a cross, but do not understand that salvation is through repentance and faith in him alone.

Facts to consider

One billion people are illiterate and must be reached either personally or by audio and visual media.

The Bible is in the languages of 93 per cent of the world's population, but most people do not have a copy.

Over 2,000 ethnic groups do not have the Scriptures in their own languages.

Millions, especially in Western countries, including Marxists and humanists, profess no religion.

Although 80 million Communist party members dominate 1.5 billion people, the gospel is spreading in Communist countries in spite of atheistic governments.

There are only 80,000 Protestant missionaries. More are needed, especially to reach Muslims and Hindus.

Most nations have some believers in Christ, but churches need to be planted among every ethnic group.

What can you do to meet the need?

7

What If I Stay?

Read Luke 12:13–34.

Aim: To understand what the Bible teaches about possessions.

Starting off

Give everyone six small cards. On each they should secretly
write down one of the most important things in their life.
They should number each card from 1 to 6, where 1 is the
most important, and 6 the least important. Place a large bin
in the middle of the group, then work through the following.

   Is any of your cards an object? It has been stolen, so bin
it.

   Is any of your cards a non-family member, a friend,
perhaps a boyfriend or a girlfriend? You have just broken
up, so throw the card away.

   Is any of your cards an ability or talent? You have just
been disabled. Discard it.

Is any of your cards a relation? They have just died. Put the card in the bin. Discuss the priorities in their lives.

Are any cards left?

Owner's manual

Read Luke 12:13–34.

Jesus talked a lot about possessions and priorities. This passage is just one of many that talks about priorities. When Jesus talked about the difficulties that possessions caused, it caused amazement among the disciples. Riches were seen as a blessing from God. Solomon in the Old Testament was greatly blessed by God in terms of material possessions, but he had the priority of seeking wisdom first (2 Chronicles 1:7–12), then the Lord added wealth and riches. The rich young ruler's problem was that he lacked one thing—Jesus. His possessions got in the way.

Jesus' statement about the difficulties of a rich man entering the kingdom of heaven is not so much a condition, but an acknowledgement of the fact that possessions can get in the way of a relationship with God. The real issue for the Christian is not how much we have, but what we do with it. Looking after the poor and needy is a responsibility laid upon those who have possessions. Whatever we have we must put to good use.

For group members

Crowdbreaker

On each of the six cards you have been given, write down one of the six most important things in your life. Then number each card from 1 to 6, where 1 is the most important thing in your life and 6 the least important. Now follow the instructions of your group leader.

Bible study

What is mine is my own. True or false?

Read Luke 12:13–34.

1. What else does life consist of? (v 15)

2. This man is described as a fool. What made him a fool?

3. In practical terms, what does this warning teach us? (v 21)

Read Genesis 2:15. What was Adam and Eve's role in the garden?

How do you feel they succeeded in looking after it?

List some of the things that God has given to you.

Read Matthew 6:31. What are 'these things'?

What is the condition attached to these being given to you?

What does 'seeking the kingdom' mean for you personally?

Real-life situation

I spend £   on myself per week.

I spend £   on God's work per week.

I give £   to a missionary organisation each week.

Be honest in your estimates.

8

Is Christianity the Only Way?

For leaders

Read John 14:6–14.

Aim: To answer the question 'Do all religions lead to God?'

Starting off

Ask the group to complete the crowdbreaker on world religions. This will help to identify how many world religions they know and what they know about them.

Owner's manual

Comparative religions are no longer an issue merely for foreign missionaries. Right here in our own country we live alongside people who hold to a different religion from our own. Religion, though, is difficult to define. For instance, Marxism is atheistic but at the same time possesses many traits of a religion such as rituals and doctrines. Is religion to do with belief in a supreme being? If so, then Buddhism is not a religion.

The Bible acknowledges that there are those who worship other 'gods', but it is more concerned to talk about the one, true, living God than playing one religion off against another. The Bible is concerned about God's interaction with his creation, his desire for a people, his revelation throughout history and his call to people to return to him. It tells us that this process came to a head in the coming of Jesus Christ—in his death and resurrection on our behalf.

It is to the claims and works of Jesus that we must look. The purpose of these studies is to show what Jesus claimed for himself and how others saw him. It is as we see this that we realise that Jesus was either mad (to claim to be God), bad (to deceive people) or he was who he said he was.

The pocket guide to religions in *Real-Life Situations* shows that even from their point of view, not all religions lead to God.

For group members

Crowdbreaker

Write down all the religions that you know and something about what they believe.

Read the following verses and write down the claims that Jesus made.

John 10:30	Mark 2:5–7
John 14:6	John 14:10

How others saw Jesus:

Matthew 16:16	Mark 1:27
1 Timothy 3:16	Matthew 8:29
Acts 4:12	

Things that Jesus did:

Luke 7:2	John 11
Mark 6:41	Matthew 8:26

Read Romans 1:18–23 and Acts 17:22–28.

What do these verses say about man's quest for God and 'religion'?

Now read Exodus 20:1–6.

What does God say about other religions?

Real-life situations

Comparative religion in a nutshell.

The Hindu Vedas said:

> *'Truth is one, but the sages speak of it in many different ways.'*

The Buddha said:

> *'My teachings point the way to the attainment of the truth.'*

Muhammad said:

> *'The truth has been revealed to me.'*

Jesus Christ said:

> *'I am the truth.'*

In this country, as well as foreign ones, we encounter those who hold different beliefs. In foreign missions Christians work in countries that are predominantly non-Christian. For instance, Bangladesh is 90 per cent Muslim. In countries like Nepal, Christians can work but not evangelise. This poses questions for us:

How do we fulfil the great commission of Matthew 28:19–20?

How do we respond when asked for our compassionate help without evangelistic activities?

9

Power for Mission

For leaders

Read Acts 1:9 and 2:1–13.

Aim: To grasp the significance of the role of the Holy Spirit for mission and evangelism.

Starting off

There is no specific crowdbreaker for this study but the following exercise brings out the *thought* of strength and weakness.

Make a circle with a radius of seven feet. Place up to a dozen guys inside it. At a given signal each tries to push everybody else out while trying to stay in himself. Once someone is pushed out of the circle, he retires from the game. The last person to stay in the circle wins.

Female supremacy

Alternatively place all the guys in a circle and have the girls surround the circle. On a given signal, the girls see how long it takes to push, pull, drag etc. all the guys from inside the circle. The guys cannot fight back in any way. They can only cling to each other for defence. If you have guys who say they are not afraid of the girls, try this and stand well back ... it's too ghastly for the printed page.

Owner's manual

A car without an engine not only won't go, but is unlikely to attract many buyers. If there is no power to drive it then it is useless. Similarly, it is one thing to have a great idea but something else to put it into action. You can have all the grandiose schemes in the world, but if you don't have the power to put them into action, then the schemes don't go anywhere.

Jesus' great commission must have seemed a huge task to the disciples. How were they going to achieve what he had asked of them? It seems even more amazing when you consider that the disciples were from unschooled backgrounds, and following the death of Jesus had all run away.

The thing that changed these timid, frightened men into men on fire for Jesus was the gift of the Holy Spirit. With all the recent debates regarding the Holy Spirit, it is sometimes forgotten why thee Holy Spirit was given—to make us effective in mission. We must also make the point that the Holy Spirit is also operating in the people to whom we go. The important thing to emphasise is not so much the ins and outs and the whys and wherefores of the gifts of the Spirit, but the purpose for which these gifts are given.

Advance warning

We suggest that in two weeks' time your youth group has a prayer concert for world mission. This will need some advance planning and preparation, so look at the notes on it before this week's session and make the appropriate preparations.

It's an Unfair World

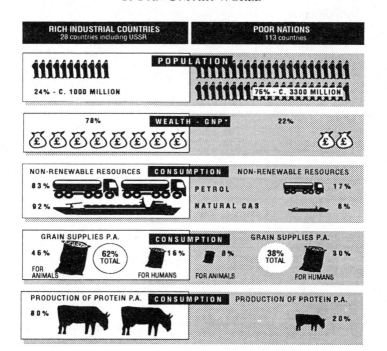

For group members

Crowdbreaker

Follow the instructions of your leader.
  Read John 20:19.
  Why were the disciples frightened?
  Read Acts 1:1–9.
  What did the disciples lack?
  What did Jesus promise them?

What was the extent of their influence to be?
Read Acts 2:1–13.
What was the reaction of the onlookers? (vv 6, 7a)
Why did they react in this way?
Read Acts 2:14.
Do you think that this was a big change for Peter?
Why? (See John 18:15–18; 25–27.)
The Holy Spirit was given to make us effective witnesses to Jesus. In the references below you will find specific things the Holy Spirit will help us with.

Luke 12:11–12.
Ability to...
John 14:17.
Ability to...
2 Corinthians 3:17–18.
Ability to...

How do you feel about this? Do you feel equipped for mission?

Mission is not just about saying the right things or even doing the right things but being the right kind of people. The Spirit helps us to develop Christlike qualities.

Read Galatians 5:22.
How would these help us in mission?
Read Luke 4:18–19.

Jesus was anointed by the Spirit to preach good news to the poor. What does this say to us about the mission in which we are involved?

Real-life situations

PERSONAL ASSESSMENT FORM

What have I learnt most about mission from this course?

What have I learnt most about myself from this course?

I have been challenged by...

My attitudes to mission:

Before this course my attitude was:

Now it is:

I intend to take further action in the following areas:

Prayer

Giving

Service with my own church

Service in this country

Service overseas

10

Am I Called?

For leaders

Read Acts 13:1–3.

Aim: To explore the concept of a call.

Starting off

Get a copy of the Highway Code and ask the group to pick several of the signs to illustrate how they feel about their life and the future. This could be an amusing exercise, but at best it will bring out the group's real feelings about guidance.

Owner's manual

Every day, people cry out for guidance. Millions of people read horoscopes to try to find a way forward. Many Christians are unaware that God has a plan for their lives. And even Christians who *are* aware often have a struggle to find out what God wants them to do. It is important to deal with this issue, to get rid of misconceptions and to help those who feel challenged as to their role in mission.

The passages in this study look at the way certain indi-

viduals were called by God. You will notice with all these
passages that the call comes in the context of worship. For
Isaiah, in individual worship, and for Paul and Barnabas,
the congregational worship of the church at Antioch. This
helps to emphasise the point, that an ongoing, healthy
relationship with God is vital if we are to make sense of
guidance. The passages referred to at the end of the Bible
study make the point that God has given us a lot of guidance already in the Bible about how we are to conduct our
lives. We should not make the mistake of thinking that we
have to be perfect in order for God to guide us, but it is
worth mentioning that guidance gets a lot easier if you are
doing the things God has already told you to do.

Advance warning

Next week we recommend you hold the prayer concert for
world mission. Make sure you look at the notes on it before
this week's session and make the appropriate preparations.

For group members

Crowdbreaker

Think about your life and the future. Flick through the
Highway Code and choose several signs that reflect how
you feel.

Bible study

Read Acts 13:1–3.

What was the church doing when God spoke? Do you
think Saul and Barnabas were important to the church at
Antioch? (Read Acts 11:19–26.) Does it surprise you that
God should call them out of the church at Antioch? Why?

Read Isaiah 6:1–8.

What did Isaiah see? (v 1) What effect did this have on

him? (v 5) How would you have felt if you had seen the same thing?

In verse 7 God touches Isaiah's life. His sin was dealt with and God asks for volunteers. Look at Isaiah's response. (v 8) Why the change around from verse 5? Why would you say 'Here I am, send me'?

The Bible teaches us that we are all called to be witnesses. The question is, what is God specifically calling me to do, and where? Before we deal with how you know God's will for your life, let us look at what God has told us in the Bible that all Christians should be doing.

We should love one another. *See John 13:34.*
We should be living a good life. *See Colossians 1:10.*
We should be speaking about Christ. *See 1 Peter 3:15.*
We should be serving one another. *See Galatians 5:13.*
We should be praying. *See Philippians 4:6–7.*

Real-life situations

Principles for guidance:

1. The Bible

This is God's revealed will for us. It tells what God wants for us. If we are contemplating doing something that we know the Bible speaks against, then we know it is not God's will for us.

2. Circumstances

Sometimes things happen that appear, on the surface, to be a coincidence. God can lead us in the right direction by events that happen in our lives.

3. God's people

The really good news is that we are not alone. God has placed us in the midst of his people, so that we can help each other.

Ask people to pray for you and to advise you. Be open to what they have to say to you.

4. Common sense

God has given you a mind so you might as well use it. If you have no obvious gift with children, then it is unlikely that God is calling you to children's work. This is not to say God doesn't call people to do extraordinary things, but more often than not, he uses logic and common sense.

5. The Holy Spirit

The inner witness of the Holy Spirit is important. This is probably the hardest factor to define and tie down. It is when God speaks to us on the inside, making us aware of how he feels. God aligns our hearts and feelings to his.

When you are seeking guidance, look for at least three of these principles to overlap and agree.

Guidance is not a tightrope that you tread carefully, going from A to B—one slip and you fall off never to get back on. The most important aspect of guidance is your relationship with God.

If you are committed to God, to getting to know him better, to serving him and doing his will, then guidance becomes that much easier. It is as our relationship grows and matures that we learn what God wants for our lives.

HELEN AND FAMILY

Oxford, England
You and Your Family
Helen (18), eldest of five children; father unemployed through ill-health; mother looking after family (ie home-work, not paid work).

Helen's story
Unemployed for six months after leaving school, then on

the Youth Training course. Your parents are unemployed, and YTS is not counted as 'work', so your family got 100% rate and rent rebate.

Your weekly budget is as follows:
YTS Training Allowance £25.50 less:
Fares (3 days a week) £3.00
To your parents (for keep) £10.00
Leaving £14.50 for everything else. If you leave the job, and go on Supplementary Benefit, your budget will be:

Supplementary Benefit £23.60 less:
To parents (no loss of rebate) £10.00
Leaving £13.60 for everything else
Choices
Do you:
1. Stay in the job?
2. Leave your job and claim Supplementary Benefit?
3. Leave home and look for a place to live?

Discuss your choices—how do you feel about the effects on you of the change from YTS to work? What will you do, and why?

Nizam Ahmed

Kusthia, W. Bangladesh
   Your family.
   Nizam Ahmed (28) and wife, Fatima (24), two boys, Fazul (8), and Sheikh (2), and two girls, Hasina (7) and Neera (5).
   Your story and important people in it:
   The Traders: retail seeds, fertilisers, pesticides, and buy harvested jute and rice. Working in a cartel they charge high prices for goods and offer low prices when farmers have to sell their crops to survive.
   The Landowner: owns ninety acres. Lives (well) in a distant town. He employs landless labourers (cheap and plentiful) to work on his best land, letting poorer land to

sharecroppers, who buy their own inputs and pay him half the harvest as rent. He is on good terms with the police and government officials.

Your story.

You, Nizam Ahmed, inherited two acres from your father, but had to surrender 1.75 acres when Neera and Sheikh were ill and you couldn't pay money for medical treatment. You became a sharecropper on half an acre, continuing to farm your remaining quarter of an acre. Last year went as follows:

January–May Planted a quarter of an acre of jute and half an acre (sharecropped) of rice. Land dry and unirrigated. *June* First rains. You hired plough and oxen, ploughed and planted, putting a minimum of expensive fertiliser on jute only. *August–September* Desperate for pesticides to save the rice crop, you borrowed money— traders had put up the price. *October–November* Half the harvest goes to landowner. To pay your debt you sold your jute immediately and cheaply. Still in debt, you sold your last quarter of an acre. This year will be similar, but now you have no savings or land.

Choices

A development agency in Bangladesh wishes to help sharecroppers. They consider these options:

1. Starting a sharecroppers' co-operative to try to break the traders' monopoly.

2. Providing a three-year supply of low-cost seeds and fertilisers for sharecroppers.

3. Paying a community worker to help you find solutions, e.g. getting access to government land (officially earmarked for the landless but in fact taken by the big landowners), or negotiating better terms for sharecropping.

Which will you choose?

11

Prayer Concert

For leaders

What is a prayer concert?

To many young people, prayer can be dull and lacking in imagination. The aim of the prayer concert is twofold:

1. It will get young people praying for the needs of the world in an imaginative way.

2. It will inform them of the needs of the world and get them to pray specifically for those needs.

We recommend your prayer concert lasts one hour. 'How,' you say, 'can I get our young people to pray for an hour?' We all know what happens when we have an open time of prayer at youth fellowship. Silence. It is probably the only time in the entire evening when there is complete quiet. The prayer concert is different. It is one hour divided up into small segments. Your time alternates between worship, information slots and prayer times. In fact, you will probably find that you need more than an hour!

This is how it works.

□ fifteen minutes of worship—ten minutes at the beginning and five minutes at the end.

□ five four-minute information slots
□ five five-minute prayer slots.

All of which equals sixty minutes!

In order for the evening to go well, you need to do some advance planning. Here is a checklist.

Worship

Choose songs, brief musicians and ensure you have word sheets, books, etc. for all the pieces you are using. Choose songs that reflect the character and sovereignty of God. Make the concert a joyful time that affirms that God is working in the world.

Prayer information slots

Choose five young people, brief them on the task, and help them with any material they need.

Ask each of your volunteers (!) to prepare four to five minutes about their given area. For instance, in slot number two, the continent is Asia. You could give a general view of Asia and then focus on one or two projects in one country. The idea is that they present two specific prayer needs and one general prayer need.

Their information can come from several sources:

□ The project material in this course.
□ Contacts in your own church—missionaries, etc.
□ Newspapers that give reports on what is happening in a particular country.
□ *Operation World* by Patrick Johnstone.
□ Missionary organisation newsletters.

Make arrangements for any audio-visual equipment that you may need.

Prayer times

Be imaginative. Split into smaller groups, divide into pairs, try times of silent prayer, use one sentence prayers. There are a whole host of ways that would make each prayer time different and interesting.

Miscellaneous

Arrange for refreshments at the end of the evening.

Make sure you have enough copies of *Around the World in Sixty Minutes*, and some spare pens.

For group members

AROUND THE WORLD IN SIXTY MINUTES

World Data 1

Continent: Europe, Country focus—
Things to pray for:
Specific needs

General needs

World Data 2

Continent: Asia, Country focus—
Things to pray for:
Specific needs

General needs

World Data 3

Continent: Australasia, Country focus—
Things to pray for
Specific needs

General needs

World Data 4

Continent: Africa, Country focus—
Things to pray for:
Specific needs

General needs

World Data 5

Continent: America, Country focus—
Things to pray for:
Specific needs

General needs

Things that I am going to continue to pray for....

12

Additional Study Material and Games

1. PREJUDICE

As soon as the third world is mentioned, people will make all kinds of remarks—some of them not based on fact, but on wrong assumptions and sometimes prejudice.

'They are poor because they are lazy.'

Try to see if you can discover any evidence for this. Who have taps in their kitchens, labour-saving devices in their homes? Who drive cars and telephone for a doctor when they are ill? Who grow their own food, carry their own water, build their own homes and work without enough food to eat?

'They are poor because they have so many children.'

The fact is that they have so many children because they are poor. A child may be the only asset they can get; more children means more hands to work on the land, and more chance of someone surviving to look after them when they are old—in the third world, there is no social security, no old age pension. Only as people get richer can they afford to have fewer children. Only as more children survive infancy can they afford to take the risk.

'They are just unlucky—it is all those natural disasters.'

Sometimes it seems that the third world has more than its fair share of natural disasters—floods, earthquakes, hurricanes. Wealthy countries have them as well; and they can afford to cope with them. In 1987 the south-east of Britain experienced hurricane-force winds—in general, trees suffered, people did not. In poor countries, not everyone has a brick-built house and an insurance policy.

'It's nothing to do with me.'

Just think of a cup of tea. The person who picked those tea leaves was probably paid less than you get in pocket money. Look at the labels on the tins of fruit in the supermarket. Rubber in car tyres, beef in burgers, cocoa in chocolate—we all have something to do with the third world every day. In that sense we live in one world—what we do affects other people, some of them thousands of miles away.

'Charity begins at home.'

We do have problems in Britain, and charity does begin at home. 99% of British charities work only in Britain—only a tiny proportion are set up to help people in other countries. A few years ago, various leaders from different countries got together and they produced what was known as The Brandt Report. They emphasised that helping the third world was not only right and good in itself, but that it was also the best thing for the rich world. Their argument was that if we ignored the third world, then in the end we would all suffer. Once again, they saw that we live in one world, and our survival is linked with their survival in all sorts of ways.

2. THE THIRD WORLD AND POVERTY

It was not intended to mean third class or third rate—like a bronze medal in the international wealth olympics. It originally meant 'a third world' in contrast to the power blocs of the West (capitalist) and the East (communist). Sometimes this third world was called the 'non-aligned nations' because they did not line up with East or West.

These same countries have also been called the undeveloped nations, the underdeveloped nations and the developing nations. All these labels suggest a judgement from others on what is happening in these countries, and puts a particular emphasis on the economies of the countries, and suggest that they are behind the rest of the world. That is why some people prefer to use the term 'two-thirds world', because it emphasises the positive importance of its size of population.

Most people, when they hear the term 'third world', think of images of poverty.

What is poverty?

How can you decide which country is poor and which is not?

It seems obvious that you would decide according to the wealth of a country. So the World Bank each year publishes a league table—richest countries at the top, poorest at the bottom. They work out something called the GNP—the Gross National Product—of each country, which roughly means all the wealth that country has created divided by the number of people in the country. Thus Ethiopia has a GNP per head of £70, compared with £6,586 in the United Kingdom.

This certainly helps to compare countries by wealth, but there are two problems:

1. These give average figures—they do not tell you how wealth is distributed in the country, how many people are

poor and how many are rich. A country might be higher in the league table, but have more poor people.

2. These figures assume poverty is only to do with wealth and money.

Some people assess poverty by what are called 'social indicators' which tell you about the quality of life rather than the quantity of money. They take into account how long people live, how many children receive education, how easy it is to get health care, how much food the people eat.

But all these things still concentrate on material, physical aspects of life. What about power, the ability to make choices and control your own life? Poverty often brings powerlessness and powerlessness brings poverty: some people suggest they are the same.

If quality of life matters more than quantity of money, then we may have to think again about the third world and poverty: the materially rich world we live in has problems—crime, drug addiction, alcoholism, pornography, broken families, unemployment, psychiatric illness. The third world has great wealth—in culture, in family and in community life.

Christians believe that these factors are related to another aspect of poverty—spiritual poverty, which results from not being in the right relationship with God, with people and with the environment.

Action

How would you define poverty? Write down your ideas or discuss them with a group.

What you think is very important, because what you think poverty is decides what you try to do about it. Make a list, by yourself or in a group, of some of the things that could be done.

Make a list of things in the third world that might make

people happy; then make a list of things in the rich world that make people sad.

3. THE POVERTY CHAIN

Tear Fund's ministry is directed at the causes of poverty in a particular community, as well as just the symptoms, so that the poverty chain can be broken, and an opportunity given to escape from the vicious circle. That is why Tear Fund gives priority to integrated development programmes which attack several links in the chain.

1. Food shortage and the wrong kind of diet are the cause of malnutrition.

2. Impure water supplies and inadequate sanitation are the major causes of poor health in the world today. 2,500 million people—half the world—have no access to clean water. 80% of all disease is related to water.

3. The combination of malnutrition and polluted water leads to poor health. A typical third world three-year-old will have had up to sixteen bouts of diarrhoea, then infections of chest and throat, an attack of measles and perhaps malaria or meningitis. Many children do not survive at all—there is a tragically high rate of infant mortality.

4. It is the uncertainty of the survival of children that encourages so many third world parents to have such large families. Children represent the possibility of wealth through an increased labour force and also security for their parents' old age. It is often in their economic interest to have large families, and so, ironically, infant mortality helps to cause rapid population growth.

5. In many rural areas large families and population increase mean that landholdings get progressively smaller as land is shared between successive generations. This results in rural poverty, with too many people trying to live off too little land.

6. One solution to this problem is to go to the towns in

search of work and wealth—a process known as urban migration. 1,000 teenagers arrive in Lima, the capital of Peru, every day.

7. Third-world towns rarely have enough paid employment to satisfy demand, so the result is high rates of unemployment, which leave many living on the informal economy of the town, things like selling food and shining shoes.

8. Unemployment, irregular employment, or simply poorly paid employment all result in low income.

9. Since the majority of the income of a poor family is spent on food, shortage of cash in the family or in the community can simply mean a food shortage.

10. The poverty chain has come full circle—the vicious circle is complete.

11. Material poverty is often reinforced by spiritual poverty. Spiritual fear and bondage often bring a fatalism or pessimism that inhibits action for development; religious beliefs and practices sometimes hinder positive change.

Action

What suggestions would you make as to how these chains could be broken?

4. THE SPIDER'S WEB

A group working in Bangladesh, supported by Tear Fund, sat down one day to think about the reality of poverty they were attempting to combat. The group were told that a baby in the village had died the day before as a result of malnutrition. They were then asked to answer the questions 'Why?' then they were to look at their answer, and ask 'Why?' again...and again...and again.... The spider's web on the following page shows all the answers they came up with.

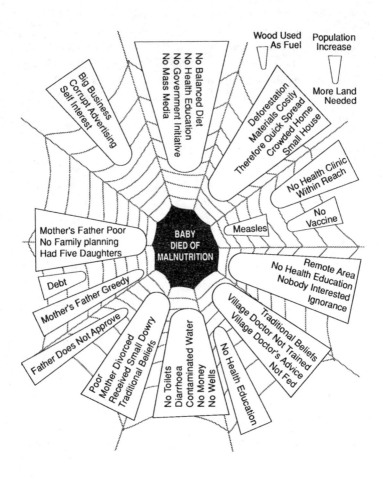

5. SLICING THE BANANA

Divide the group into six equal units. Name the groups pickers, retailers, wholesalers, importers, shippers and packers. Put a blank cardboard banana on the wall with a

10p tag, and ask the groups to negotiate the percentage each should get for their labour and costs.

After five minutes get each group to present its case. Write the amounts on the blank banana. Get them to adjust their claims until it equals 10p. Then reveal the actual situation:

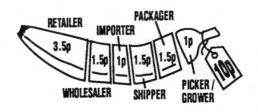

1. How do the two sets of divisions compare?
2. How do the pickers feel?
3. Which does the group feel is the fairest division of price?
4. Can the group think of a way to give the pickers and growers a better share?

Christian Aid has produced a thirty-minute filmstrip about banana production in the Dominican Republic, called *Banana Split*. The filmstrip comes complete with notes and discussion questions.

6. WATER

Water is top of Tear Fund's priority list—helping people obtain a clean, regular and free supply of water can break the poverty chain. A poor water supply means hardship and disease; an improved water supply can make all the difference.

EFICOR is one of Tear Fund's partners—it is a very similar organisation to Tear Fund, evangelical Christians working together in India to follow Jesus and help people in need. Tear Fund has supported the EFICOR well-drilling team for many years.

In order to get the heavy drilling vehicles into some villages, roads have to be laid, as the lorries cannot go far from the main roads. Before they start drilling, the crew of six men pray for God's blessing on their work, and then the generator starts up, with a deafening noise, and the drill begins to bite into the soil and rock. Somewhere, usually about 150 feet down, they hit water and to the great excitement of the village, it comes gushing out of the ground. Then a pump is fixed, and clean water becomes available.

Meet two people who have seen the drilling rig come and make a big difference to their lives.

Munjula

Munjula was twelve years old. Every day she would get up at five o'clock, collect the large water pot and carry it on her head for the long walk to the only well in the village. Often she would have to wait for the higher-status women to finish. Then, after breakfast, she would go to school, unless her mother was working and she had to look after her baby brother. In the afternoon, she would make two further trips to the well, carrying her baby brother and the water pot.

Munjula lived in Melputhupakam in a dry area of India, where it had not rained for five years, and the well was beginning to dry up. After the drilling rig came, there was a new well, with a pump, giving plenty of clean water—and it was much closer to her house in the poor part of the village.

Noel

Noel's story is not so happy. He lived in a village called Vilapakkam where his father was the village school teacher. Noel's family were Christians, living in the poorest part of the village, where they had to get their water from a tank controlled by the wealthier people in the area. They looked down on the poorest group, and made it difficult for them to get their water. Noel's father worked hard to help the villagers get the water from the richer people that the government said they should have—and one night he was beaten and murdered, and the houses in Noel's part of the village were all set on fire. All this because of the dispute over water.

EFICOR heard of this situation, and came to drill a well in Noel's part of the village. Those who had killed his father were not very happy to see their power being taken away— because once they did not control the water supply they could not control the poor people so easily. So when the well was drilled and the pump fitted, it not only helped the poor people's health, but also set them free from the injustice and oppression of the wealthier part of the village.

Action

See if you can write a diary describing how you would feel about a new well being drilled in your village. Think of it in three stages—getting ready, seeing it happen, and the difference it would make.

7. WATER, WATER!

1 When you boil the kettle for one cuppa do you:

a Fill it up to the top?
b Fill it no more than a third full?

c Not bother to look?

2 You decide to have a bath. Do you:

a Fill the bath near to the top so it overflows when you get in it?
b Keep the water level just over your knees?
c Start with the water level just over your knees but keep the tap running?

3 The car needs washing. Do you:

a Offer to clean it and use the hose pipe on full?
b Use two or three buckets and plenty of elbow grease?
c Nip down to the garage car wash?

Answers:
All 'A's. Oh dear. You wouldn't survive very long if there was a water shortage. All Bs. Brilliant. We need more people like you. All Cs. Danger zone. If everyone was like you there would be a water shortage.

8. CHARITY VERSUS JUSTICE

Aim: to understand that, although charity is good, to bring about real change we need to challenge the deeper roots of injustice.
   You will need...
   A set of photos and posters
   Sticky dots of different colours
   Paper and pencils

Variant A Time required: fifteen minutes
   Obtain a range of photos or posters. Photo sets are available from Christian Aid and other agencies. (Back copies of Christian Aid calendars may be useful.)
   Stick pictures up on the wall and give each pair of young

people three different colour sticky dots, or coloured paper tokens and Blue-tac. Ask each pair to rank the photos according to which makes most impression on them, and to place their dots accordingly, e.g. yellow, most impression; blue, next; red, next. Give them five to ten minutes and then talk about the results.

Variant B Time required twenty minutes

Now ask two pairs to combine and take the pictures off the wall. Give one to each group (use the highest rated ones if you have a choice). In addition give each group of four a sheet of paper and pencils. Ask them to begin asking questions about the photo and write down their questions.

Why does she look sad? What is he drinking? Where are they? What is she thinking? Is he her husband or her father? Why is he so thin? And so on.

Variant C

As a bit of light relief you could put the photos back on the wall, and ask the group to make up silly captions—give a prize to the most original.

After ten minutes ask whether their attitude to the photo has changed.

Do we dismiss things at face value too often?

Is it useful to ask questions?

9. PLANNING EFFECTIVE PRAYER FOR THE WORLD

'... And please God, bless all the missionaries.'

How often have we heard such a prayer? The intention may have been good, but the likelihood of any result coming from it is minimal.

Prayer for the world is vital. 'Prayer is fundamental in the kingdom of God. It is not an optional extra, nor is it a last resort when all other methods have failed.' (Patrick Johnstone)

'As far as God can go—geographically, culturally, spiritually—prayer can go. Our requests actually touch people where they are because God is there to touch them according to what we ask.' (David Bryant)

Personal preparation is essential

1. Prayer for the world must flow from concern for God's glory to be seen in all the world.

2. Preparation time for intercession for the world in church services is just as important as preparation for preaching. Adequate information based on careful research must be accompanied by a compassionate identification with those for whom you are praying.

3. Use your imagination to recognise the plight of the hopeless, the despair of those in war zones, the temptations of the prisoner, the heartache of the missionary mother saying goodbye to a child returning to boarding school.

4. Recruit helpers to monitor particular countries with which your church is involved. Invite different members of the church to take mission magazines or letters from overseas with specific requests or praise items.

5. Make full use of media coverage. TV pictures, newspaper headlines and magazine articles can all provide valuable ways of relating to the world around us.

Intercession for the world in Sunday services

1. Make this a natural and regular feature of your prayers. We now live in a global village. What happens in the Gulf, in Brussels, in Moscow, now affects our lives in one way or another.

2. When disaster strikes in another part of the world, pray for Christians there who will be affected. We belong to

the one church: we are part of the same body of Christ. Let us identify ourselves as such through prayer.

3. Inspire others to pray for the world through your example.

4. Involve others who know certain missionaries in leading in prayer for them. Use the overhead projector to identify the country or city for which you are praying. Write up key names and brief requests so people can more easily remember the specific items for prayer.

5. Pray for nations of the world and their leaders. (1 Timothy 2:1–3)

6. Pray for church leaders around the world. They often request prayer for their ministry. A good rule to adopt is to pray for a national Christian as often as you pray for any missionary with whom your church is linked. It is vital to continue to pray for the church leaders after the missionary from your church has returned to his home country.

Special prayer times for the world

Make these times exciting and popular by observing these basic rules:

1. Format

The more accustomed we become to routine, the less vital it is to us. Sometimes begin the meeting with worship followed by intercession and thanksgiving; other times with a brief challenge to prayer. If ministry from the Bible is given, make it short yet powerful. Experiment with various formats and you will find people will be helpful in suggesting others.

Incorporating times of worship in the prayer time draws us into God's presence, where our faith is strengthened and released to believe him for great answers to prayer!

2. Delegation

Ask individuals in advance to give a brief update on a particular country. This is part of effective preparation. This could include statistics (from *Operation World* for example) about a particular country or religion of the world.

Newspapers are full of prayer needs related to the world and the plight of the lost, living in ignorance and fear. These can be an excellent source of prayer material and someone can read directly from clippings collected in preparation for the meeting.

3. Map

In order to encourage people to become more worldwide in their vision, make regular use of a world map or the overhead projector with well-drawn acetates depicting various continents of the world.

4. Encouragement

Urge different people to pray. Help everyone to feel relaxed in terms of grammar, theological content or length. Especially encourage those who don't pray very often or not at all, but don't embarrass anyone!

5. Variation

Use parts of films, videos, slides or filmstrips whenever possible and applicable. Many mission groups have produced very effective and informative audio-visual aids that are a good stimulus to prayer.

When using audio-visuals, stop for a time of prayer after each section. This also makes the prayer time a learning experience which, in turn, stimulates the participation.

6. Participation

Prayer must involve the mind as well as the heart. Long periods without personal involvement allow the mind to drift. Break into groups of three to five people during times of prayer so that each person is given an opportunity to participate.

Each group could be given information about one area of need and be asked to concentrate their prayers on that, or all could pray in groups for the same needs. Break into several different-sized groups during the prayer meeting.

7. *Prayer requests*

Keep prayer requests short when they are presented. Long, detailed accounts for prayer not only kill the spirit of the meeting but they also often leave very little time for prayer!

Some items for prayer and praise could be written in advance and given out to people as they arrive or they could be written on a black-board as they are presented. An overhead projector is helpful to outline maps of various countries or to display prayer requests which have been recorded. (A set of OHP transparencies of many countries of the world is available from WEC International, Bulstrode, Gerrards Cross, Bucks SL9 8SZ.)

8. *Answers*

Keep a record of prayer needs. If you are believing for and expecting specific answers to prayer, you will want to encourage your pray-ers with specific answers to prayer.

Conclusion

Remember, you are not just praying for the work, prayer is the work—hard labour in fact! Above all, may we discover that prayer for the world is outward-looking, captive-releasing, kingdom-taking and Christ-glorifying.

Books on praying for the world

Operation World
A day-to-day guide to praying for the world.

Patrick Johnstone.
STL/WEC.

Touch the World through Prayer
This explains how every Christian can pray for missionaries, church leaders and political leaders in countries around the globe.
Wesley L. Duewel
Francis Asbury Press/Zondervan.

Key to the Missionary Problem
This book sounds a rousing and solemn call to fresh activity and more abundant prayer for the cause of missions.
Andrew Murray.
Christian Literature Crusade.

Mountain Rain
This new biography of James O. Fraser documents how the prayers of God's people brought a harvest many thousands of miles away.
Eileen Crossman.
OMF/STL.

World Church Sunday Resource Pack
Produced by the Evangelical Missionary Alliance, Whitefield House, 186 Kennington Park Road, London SE11 4BT.

10. COUNTRY FILE

1. BANGLADESH

Area: 144,000 sq km (formerly East Pakistan)
   Population: 98 million
   Language: Bengali (official). English is spoken by most well-educated people.

Religion: 85 per cent are Muslim, but there are many Hindu, Buddhist and Christian.

Education: Although there are universities and colleges in Bangladesh, only 20 per cent of the country's people are capable of passing a simple literacy test. At present only 36 per cent of children over six attend any kind of school.

Health: Every ten minutes, sixty babies are born in Bangladesh but at least twelve of these will die before they are five. Life expectancy is only forty-eight because few people have been vaccinated against common diseases. Only a small minority has access to clean water. People here rely on their children to support them in their old age, and so want large families to ensure that at least some of their children will reach adulthood.

Income: Bangladesh is one of the world's poorest countries. The Gross National Product is only £98 per capita, per annum (Britain's is £6,586). It is estimated that 86 per cent of the population cannot afford the basic necessities of life and are living beyond the absolute poverty level.

Church involvement: Missions have been welcomed for their social uplift programmes. Since 1980 increased limitations have been placed on missionaries with all projects, plans and finances needing government approval. The church has been plagued by nominalism, spiritual shallowness, inferiority (almost all are from low-caste Hinduism or minority tribal peoples).

2. INDIA

Area: 33,287,593 sq km.

Population: 816.8 million (1988). 75% live in rural communities.

Life expectancy is 56 years (U.K. 75 years).

Access to safe drinking water:
Urban population 80% (U.K. 100%);
Rural population 47% (U.K. 100%).

Education: Children start school when they are six; however, only half of India's children actually attend school—many are too poor to pay for school books and uniforms. Others desperately need the small amounts their young children can earn by working. Half of India's adults are illiterate.

Health: One hundred and twenty children in every thousand die before their first birthday (Europe 11 in 1,000). Less than half of India's people have access to clean drinking water, so diarrhoea, dysentery and intestinal disease are rife. Diseases such as polio are still common.

Religion: India is a secular state which grants constitutional freedom to all religions to practise and to spread their faith. Hinduism is by far the strongest religion in the country, claiming about 82 per cent of the population. Other religions include:

> Muslims 11 per cent
> Christians 3 per cent
> Sikhs 2 per cent

Approximately 0.7 per cent of Indians are evangelical Christians, many belonging to the Evangelical Fellowship of India, a body of more than 100 evangelical organisations. The Fellowship is particularly active in promoting both evangelism and social action in needy areas of the country.

Income: India's Gross National Product is £150 per capita, per annum (in Britain this is £6,586). Because employment is scarce, people are willing to work extremely long hours for a very low wage. Many people work in iron and steel mills under worse conditions than those of Victorian England. More than half of the population live below the absolute poverty level. Many homeless people are born, live and die on India's city streets.

13

Audio-Visual Guide

This is in no way intended to be an exhaustive guide to video and other resources. Those listed here are thought to be particularly suited to this course. All prices are subject to revision. A fuller list of resources can be found from the following organisations:

Tear Fund

Resources Catalogue available from:
    Tear Fund
    100 Church Road
    Teddington
    Middlesex
    TW11 8QE

Christian Aid

Resources List available from:
    Christian Aid
    PO Box 100
    London
    SE1 7RT

140 CHRISTMAS CRACKER

Interserve

Resources available from Nishi Sharma, address as for
WORM.

WORM

(World Outreach Resource Material) available from:
    Evangelical Missionary Alliance
    Whitefield House
    186 Kennington Park Road
    London SE11 4BT
A comprehensive list of what is available to interest
children and young people in mission.

Films

The Living City (Christian Aid) thirty minutes. 1977
    More than 2.5 million people live in the slums of Cal-
cutta, one family to a hut about twelve feet square. Conditions in Calcutta, where half a million daily cross the
Howrah bridge to the city's centre, are notorious. Less well
known are the positive efforts made by Calcutta's people,
with the help of government and voluntary agencies, to
create a better future for themselves.
    Besides outlining its many problems, the film describes
the hopeful, living face of Calcutta. Also available in
35 mm format for use in cinemas. Holder of the British
Academy Award for the best short factual film of 1977.
Age: fourteen years and over.

Videos

The vast majority of the videos listed here can be hired.
Therefore, we have included hiring details of various
organisations. It is also worthwhile checking with your local
Christian bookshop as they may have the titles in stock,
available to you for hire.

Christmas Cracker: A different kind of giving (Oasis/*21CC*)
twenty minutes. 1990

With Steve Chalke, and featuring Phil Collins 'Another
Day in Paradise'. In this video, shot in the UK, Uganda and
India, Steve Chalke tells the remarkable story of Christmas
Cracker 1989, and encourages young people to get involved
in the project.

Yonder Peasant (Christian Aid) twenty-two minutes. 1987
(Video filmstrip)

Sir Michael Hordern narrates this fantasy, a development parable loosely based on the story of Good King
Wenceslas, which deepens the King's understanding of
poverty—and our own. Age: thirteen years and over.

Diagnosis Poverty (Christian Aid) fifteen minutes. 1982

This programme explains how the health of the poor in
countries like Bangladesh is rooted in the more fundamental problems of poverty and landlessness. Nizam, a para-
medic, was murdered in his own village of Shimulia because
he tried to ask the basic question: why are the people poor?
The varied work of voluntary agencies in seeking com-
munity-based solutions is described in detail. Age: fourteen
years and over.

No Choices (Tear Fund) eighteen minutes.

Popular Christian rock musician Martyn Joseph visits
Thailand to see for himself the reality of life in the third
world. He meets people in their homes, entertains children
in schools and walks the streets of Bangkok after dark,
seeing for himself the scale of the problems and being
heartened by the way Christians are seeking solutions. He
sings a number of songs, including the title track 'No
Choices', and shares his reactions freely and frankly with
the camera.

Women Like Us (Tear Fund) twenty-seven minutes.

Three women living in great poverty in Ecuador tell the story of their daily struggle against poverty and share their dreams for the future. Interspersed between each story are interviews with women in Britain talking about their reactions to situations of poverty. Shot on location in Ecuador and Britain, it is ideal for use in home groups, especially among women, challenging attitudes and shaping responses. It won a Gold Camera Award at the United States Industrial Film and Video Festival. Leaders' Notes suggest questions for discussion and give hints on how to handle the presentation.

It's a Small World (Tear Fund) thirty-two minutes.

Cliff Richard narrates this award-winning account of Tear Fund's child sponsorship programmes in Haiti. He sees for himself the problems faced by children growing up in the poorest country in the western hemisphere—and the difference which sponsorship can make to whole communities.

Partners (Tear Fund) eighteen minutes (Video filmstrip)

An ideal introduction to Tear Fund's ministry which shows how the concept of partnership is fundamental to its work at home and overseas, and how in the global community rich and poor need to work together to ensure our common survival. The filmstrip describes how Tear Fund co-operates with its partners overseas to help people survive disasters, to set them on the road to long-term recovery, to tackle issues of social justice and to introduce those being helped to the love of Christ.

Jesus Commands Us to Go (WORM) eight minutes

Very challenging—ideal to motivate young people into active involvement in world mission. Based on the Keith Green song of the same name.

Available from: SIM International, Joint Mission Centre, Ullswater Crescent, Coulsden, Surrey, CR3 2HR.

Word in Action (Tear Fund) nineteen minutes (Video filmstrip)

A teaching filmstrip in which John Stott, Tear Fund's president, expounds the biblical basis for social concern, showing how Jesus met spiritual and physical needs with love and compassion, and how Tear Fund-supported programmes in Peru, Kenya, Bangladesh and Nepal seek to follow his example. Includes outline Bible study.

City Vision (Tear Fund) thirteen minutes (Video filmstrip)

This lively, fast-moving video version of a very popular filmstrip includes film shot at a concert by the Christian East End funk and reggae band 'Cityvision' who are committed to evangelism and practical care in inner London. Their concern for London is matched by that of Christian groups in slum areas of Calcutta and Nairobi who, as in the filmstrip, are shown bringing help and healing to young and old. The video also includes some exciting computer graphics. The original filmstrip version is still available.

Survival (Tear Fund) seventeen minutes (Video filmstrip)

This exciting video version of a highly-acclaimed filmstrip tells the story of two teenagers playing a computer game called 'Survival' who suddenly find themselves transported into the real situation the game describes. Computer graphics enliven the superb artwork of the original filmstrip showing them at work on a Bangladesh tea estate, catching typhoid from contaminated milk and perishing in floods en route to the nearest doctor. Back in the real world again they realise just how unfair life in the third world generally is, and determine to do something about it. The original filmstrip is still available.

Where There's Hope, There's Life (Tear Fund) eighteen minutes

This filmstrip shows why millions of people are flocking to the world's major cities with little hope of shelter, work or even survival, and how Tear Fund's partners in Delhi and Calcutta are seeking to meet the needs of the poor.

Healing Hands (Interserve).

Up-to-date story of the first wholly indigenous medical missionary society—the Emmanuel Hospitals Association in India. Shot in four Indian states, this moving and powerful testimony shows the healing power of the gospel. Ideal for contemporary perspective on missions. Suitable for fourteen and over. For hire. Contributions only.

Resource materials

The Poverty Chain (Tear Fund) £5.95

A powerful presentation of the interrelated causes of poverty in the world and their consequences in human suffering. Twelve two-colour acetate sheets contain graphic images illustrating the problems, and detailed fact sheets provide background information and examples of Tear Fund's response. The pack also includes the Poverty Chain Set.

The Development Game (Tear Fund) £5.00

Much more than just a game, it offers a profound learning experience for all who take part (any number between sixteen and seventy). Everyone takes on the role of an African villager or member of a visiting development team. They act out their role according to the information on the character card they are given, and discuss the village's needs and the development team's suggested action. It comes complete with ninety character cards, a slide set with taped commentary, map posters, instructions and information sheets.

Water of Life (Tear Fund) £5.95

Posters, stickers, background information about water problems in developing countries, suggestions for group activity, worship material for Sunday services and sample leaflets for general use with young people. Also includes an attractive overhead projector presentation with eight full-colour transparencies exploring the theme of water—its abundance and life-giving qualities on the one hand; and on the other its scarcity and dangerous nature in many parts of the third world.

At Your Service (Tear Fund) £2.95

A selection of activity ideas, background information sheets, posters and other material on the general theme of relief and development, taken from special focus packs in the past.

Student Pack (Tear Fund) £2.00

Designed to help students understand the causes and consequences of world poverty and how they can respond through the various ministries of Tear Fund.

It's Not Fair (Christian Aid) £3.00

An A4 handbook on world development for youth leaders, comprising sixteen sections each of which gives practical suggestions for a session or workshop with young people on a specific topic. Issues dealt with include lifestyle, peace and unemployment and there are many ideas for action. Each section ends with a sheet of worship resources.

We Ask Why They Are Hungry? (Christian Aid) £5.00

A teachers' pack for GCSE jointly produced by Christian Aid and CAFOD. It explores a Christian response to world poverty through games, role plays, worksheets, maps and real-life stories.

The Trading Game (Christian Aid) 50p
This lively game for fifteen to thirty players aged fourteen and over can be used to help the players understand how trade affects national prosperity. Playing time ninety minutes.

The Paper Bag Game (Christian Aid) 50p
How many paper bags can you make in order to live? The aim of this game for ten to thirty-five players aged ten and over is to simulate the pressures of trying to survive in an economy like Calcutta's, where there is massive unemployment and no social security. Playing time fifty minutes.

Fair Play (Christian Aid) 30p
A role play about justice based on true stories from Bangladesh, Nicaragua, South Africa and the UK.

Farming For a Future (World Vision) £7.50
A world development activity pack for secondary schools.
Available from:
World Vision of Britain
Dychurch House
8 Abington Street
Northampton
NN1 2AJ

Practically speaking

To book a video...
From Tear Fund
Tear Fund videos are available only in VHS format for

purchase at £9.95, or for hire at £3.00 per week. For details, contact Tear Fund, 100 Church Road, Teddington, Middlesex, TW11 8QE.

From Christian Aid

At least fourteen days' notice is requested for all bookings. Please phone if time is short. Filmstrips and videos of filmstrips are loaned free of charge. They are also available to buy: £10 per filmstrip; £25 per video.

Showing an audio-visual

1. Run through all materials as long before showing as possible to ensure you are familiar with them and that everything is in order. Give yourself time to get any problems put right.

2. Make sure equipment is clean and in good working order, especially parts that may damage the audio-visual itself.

3. Check extension leads, spare bulbs, screen, power points, projector stand. Poor blackout ruins films and filmstrips. Avoid compromises by thinking ahead. Get the room ready well before people arrive.

4. Remember that people in a room absorb sound, so you need to be able to turn up the volume when you actually start the showing.

Videos

Check that there is no reflected light on the TV screen and that it can be seen by all. Beware of attempting to turn up sound on a domestic TV set so much that it becomes distorted. Such a set can only really cope with a maximum of fifty people in a small hall. For larger rooms, it is relatively simple to arrange for two TV sets to run off a single video player. Ask for advice at your local electric shop.

Films

Make particular efforts to clean the gate so that the film is not damaged. Position the speaker close to the screen and at a good height. Make sure people have a good view of the screen—a high screen also means a high projector stand.

Filmstrips

Small domestic cassette recorders are inadequate in large halls. Make sure that you can amplify the sound sufficiently for it still to be clear when the room is full. Showing a filmstrip often requires two people—one to adjust the sound, and one to turn the filmstrip. A torch assists you to read the script; a run-through really does help!

Further Reading

Finding Your Way
Martin and Elizabeth
Goldsmith
STL £1.50

Getting There From Here
Elizabeth Goldsmith
STL £1.95

Love Your Local Missionary
Edited by Martin Goldsmith
STL £2.25

Through Gates of Splendour
Elisabeth Elliot
STL £2.50

*William Carey: By Trade a
Cobbler*
Kellsye M Finnie
STL £1.95

I Dared to Call Him Father
Bilquis Sheikh
Kingsway £2.25

The Challenge of Missions
Oswald J Smith
STL £2.50

Friendship Across Culture
Tim Stafford
STL £3.95

*God's Mission: Healing The
Nations*
David Burnett
Marc/STL £2.75

Ishmael My Brother
Edited by Anne Cooper
Marc/STL £4.95

*Jesus And The World
Religions*
Ajith Fernando
Marc/STL £2.50

Operation World
Patrick Johnstone
STL £4.50

Ripening Harvest, Gathering Storm
Maurice Sinclair
Marc/STL £3.95

Ten Sending Churches
Edited by Michael Griffiths
Marc/STL £2.25

The World Christian Starter Kit
Glenn Myers
STL £1.50

Concise Guide to Today's Religions
Josh McDowell and Don Stewart
Scripture Press £7.95

Who is my Neighbour? World Faiths and Christian Witness
Martin Goldsmith and Rosemary Harley
Scripture Union £4.25

Evangelism—Now and Then
Michael Green
IVP

A Hitch-Hiker's Guide to Mission
Ada Lum
STL/IVP £1.75

Christians And The Third World
David Edgington
The Paternoster Press Ltd
£4.00

Third World Conundrum
Max Peberdy
The Paternoster Press £2.95

Images From An African Journey
Mark Patinkin
The Paternoster Press £3.95

Poor Is No Excuse
John Allan
The Paternoster Press £2.50

A Lion Handbook to The World's Religions
Lion Publishing £7.50

Don't Soft-Pedal God's Call
Michael Griffiths
OMF £0.60

The Final Frontier
McClung, Blessitt and others
Kingsway £2.25

Get Your Church Involved in Mission
Michael Griffiths
OMF £0.60

So I Send You
John Marsh
Marc £2.95

Keep in Touch

We've told you the Why and the How. Now *21CC* magazine gives you the Who, What and When.

Each month we'll help you relate your faith to current issues,
- with down-to-earth projects like Christmas Cracker,
- bring you perceptive Bible teaching from Christian leaders like Floyd McClung,
- keep you in the picture with news, reviews, interviews and analysis,
- practical ideas for your youth group from Steve Chalke month by month, and of course regular updates on Christmas Cracker.

To make sure of your own copy each month ask at your local Christian bookshop or, in case of difficulty, write to: 21CC, 37 Elm Road, New Malden, Surrey KT3 3HB.

I would like to know more about registering my youth group for Christmas Cracker. Please send me details.

Name ....

Address ....

....

....

Tel No. ....

Please return this form, or write to:

Christmas Cracker
Haddon Hall Baptist Church
Tower Bridge Road
London
SE1 4TR

NOTES